CU00847953

NATIONAL
GEOGRAPHIC
KiDS

ULTIMATE
Explorer
FIELD GUIDE

NATIONAL GEOGRAPHIC
WASHINGTON, D.C.

GREYLAG GOOSE p. 15

AVOCET p. 46

PEREGRINE p. 77

Contents

BLUE TIT p. 84

STARLING p. 99

GOLDFINCH p. 120

LET'S GO Birding!

BIRDING IS LIKE A TREASURE HUNT. Every time you go outside—whether it's into your garden or into the countryside—you can discover a winged wonder. Ask yourself: What's out there today? What will I find? Then look into the sky to see a tiny Swift somersaulting through the air to catch an insect for dinner. Look down to see a Dunnock hopping about under the bird table picking up the seeds other birds have knocked to the ground. Look into the trees to discover a nest filled with Robin babies' open beaks, waiting for their mum to return with food. Look across a lake or marsh to see a huge Grey Heron flapping its massive wings in flight, like an ancient flying dinosaur. Why do we love to watch birds? Of all the animals in nature, birds are the easiest to find and enjoy. About 10,000 species have been named around the world, with 300 or so regular or occasional visitors to the UK. Each year many people enjoy watching birds either outside in the wild, in dedicated reserves, or just simply through their windows. You might want to join them! You can get started right now with a tour of the 200 bird species in this book. It's a fairly comprehensive list with all of the species you are likely to see described and photographed. You'll find all kinds—from tiny, beautifully coloured tits and finches, to huge predators like the majestic Golden Eagle. The birds appear in their taxonomic order—the way they are ranked by family in the animal kingdom—as endorsed by the British Trust for Ornithology. A good way to see birds quickly is to put out a bird feeder. Soon you'll be identifying its visitors. As you locate each bird in this book, be sure to keep a list, and add to it throughout the year. Soon you'll call yourself a birdwatcher, or a birder for short. Welcome to the club!

— The Editors

HOW TO USE This Book

GET OUTSIDE! LOOK AROUND! Take this book with you! Use the many special features of this field guide to discover how to spot birds and pick up expert tips.

Bird Entry

THIS IS WHERE YOU'LL FIND THE BIRD'S COMMON NAME.

BIRD'S SCIENTIFIC NAME.

HERE ARE SOME STATISTICS AND INFORMATION ABOUT THE BIRD, SUCH AS ITS AVERAGE LENGTH, ITS WINGSPAN, THE FOOD IT EATS AND THE HABITAT IT PREFERS.

PHOTOGRAPH OF THE BIRD SHOWING SOME OF ITS KEY FEATURES OR MARKINGS.

SPARKLE ARROWTAIL AND TAIL FEATHERS

HOBBY

Falco subbuteo
LENGTH 28–36cm   WINGSPAN 70–90cm
WEIGHT 130–340g   HABITAT Farmland, heathland
and open grassland   FOOD Small birds and insects

THIS BIRD OF prey is around the same size as a Kestrel, and is fairly magnificent in flight. It dashes and darts, chasing smaller birds and large insects. It will often grasp its catch with its talons initially, and transfer it to its beak whilst gliding through the air.

THIS TEXT GIVES YOU A GENERAL DESCRIPTION OF THE SPECIES, INCLUDING KEY BEHAVIOURS, HUNTING AND EATING HABITS, AND SOME SURPRISING FACTS.

LONG, NARROW WINGS

USE THESE LABELS TO QUICKLY IDENTIFY A SPECIES. CAN YOU NAME IT IN 10 SECONDS?

LARGE YELLOW FEET WITH DARK GREY OR BLACK TIP

PEREGRINE

Falco peregrinus
LENGTH 39–50cm   WINGSPAN 95–115cm   WEIGHT 600g–1.3kg
HABITAT Marshland and coastal wetlands   FOOD Medium-
sized birds including ducks and pigeons

THIS FAST-FLYING, anchor-shaped falcon feeds mainly on birds such as pigeons and doves, which it catches in flight. When it swoops down on its victim it becomes the fastest creature in the world!

SELECTED ENTRIES HAVE ADDITONAL COOL FACTS THAT TELL YOU SOMETHING EXTRA ABOUT THAT PARTICULAR SPECIES.

LARGE FEET WITH SHARP TALONS

be a BIRD NERD!

The "stoop" or dive of the Peregrine can achieve a speed of over 200mph. It is travelling so fast that the Peregrine purposely aims to the side of its victim as a direct hit at that speed could damage the falcon almost as much as its prey.

FALCONS (FALCONIDAE)   **9**

Birdtastics Features

BIRDTASTICS PAGES show species that share unique habitats, strange behaviours or special features.

TEXT BLOCKS GIVE INFORMATION ABOUT THE FEATURED HABITAT, BEHAVIOUR OR SPECIES.

A CAPTION DESCRIBES THE MAIN PHOTO.

DISCOVER HABITATS LIKE THE OPEN OCEAN AND FIND OUT WHAT KINDS OF BIRDS LIVE THERE.

Classification

BIRD SPECIES ARE GROUPED TOGETHER IN FAMILIES

based on their physical characteristics and genetic makeup. This classification is called taxonomy, and scientific family names are written in Latin. Birds in this book are arranged by the families they belong in. The common family names, along with the scientific ones, can be found at the bottom of the pages.

TAXONOMY TAB

GETTING STARTED:
Field Tricks & Tips

IF YOU LIKE TO LOOK AT BIRDS, read more about them, learn how to identify species, then you're ready to be a birder! Here are a few things you can do to get started.

Where to Find Them

Birds are everywhere. That's the great thing about being a birder—you can walk right out the front door and start looking! You'll soon find that specific kinds, or species, of birds live in specific habitats—the climate, landscape and plant life of a place. For instance, you might see a Blue Tit in your garden but you're more likely to see a Buzzard in the countryside. That's because different places offer things that specific birds need to survive: food, protection from predators, and a safe spot for nesting. So when you go looking for a bird, first think about the habitat you might find it in. A Barn Owl lives in—you guessed it!—a barn and other big buildings where it can make a nest and be close to open fields that have plenty of mice and other small mammals for food. So if you're around a farm, take a look for a Barn Owl. Some birds aren't easy to spot, but if you know the habitat they live in you can be on the alert!

Each bird entry in this book describes the bird's habitat. Some stay in one place all year round. Others migrate, or fly to different places at different times

of the year, so their range is wide and their type of habitat can vary.

What They Look Like

Birders need to pay attention to details! Whether you're watching a bird sitting on a fence outside your window or you're looking through a pair of binoculars at a bird in flight, know what to look for. A bird's "field marks" tell you something unique about the bird that will help you identify it. Here are the most important things to look for when trying to identify a bird:

- ✓ Colour
- ✓ Colour patterns
- ✓ Size
- ✓ Shape
- ✓ Behaviour
- ✓ Song
- ✓ Habitat
- ✓ Geographical range

Identifying just two or three of these items will help you significantly narrow down a bird species. Sometimes the only difference between two species is a slight variation in a marking. For that reason, it's good to have your field guide handy when you're out looking for birds. Also, be sure to take a mental picture of a bird you spot. Try to remember as many details as possible and write them in a

Golden Eagle

notebook so you can recognise that bird in the future.

Here's an important thing to know about bird identification: males and females of the same species can look very different. Males often have the more colourful feathers! So it's good to know what the male and female of a particular species look like. To make matters even more challenging, some birds have different colour patterns during different times of the year. During certain times, birds go through a process called moulting, when they lose old feathers and grow new ones—and the timing is different for different birds. No one said birding was going to be simple!

What to Listen For

Songs and notes are another clue to help you identify a bird. Bird species have a unique song or call, which can be a sure giveaway for identifying that species. Sometimes you'll hear a song first, like a Mourning Dove's *oowoo-woo-woo-woo*, and then you can follow the song to the bird.

Be a Bird Lover

When you spend time watching birds, you quickly gain respect for how beautiful, powerful, smart and graceful they are. They're also sensitive. Here are a few things you need to know:

Cats that prey on birds and their nests have driven down bird populations in some areas. To help protect birds, keep cats indoors.

Birds are very sensitive to pollutants and pesticides. Talk to your parents about avoiding the use of chemicals to control pests in your garden. Insects are important food for birds!

Birds can be injured or killed when they become entangled in plastic bags and plastic packaging. Before recycling

or discarding plastic bags, tie them in a knot. Cut open plastic soda rings so a bird's head can't get stuck in it.

Winter can be a tough time of year for our feathered friends when it comes to finding food. Put up bird feeders in the winter to help out birds that are in your garden year-round. Keep the feeders clean and make sure to hang them in a spot that squirrels and cats can't reach.

✓ CHECKLIST FOR BIRDERS
Want to be a pro bird-watcher? Here's a checklist to get you started.

✓ **BRING BINOCS**
A good pair of binoculars is a must for birding. First use your naked eye to scan for birds, and then bring the binoculars up for a closer view. It's hard to scan an area through the magnified lenses.

✓ **GET A GOOD GUIDE**
Be sure to bring this book on your hikes or car trips. But since there are only 200 birds in this book and space is limited you might want to check the RSPB website to see examples of some of the rarer species.

✓ **MAKE A NOTE OF IT**
Grab a small spiral notebook and a pen or pencil for your backpack. You'll find out more about the importance of taking notes on page 13.

✓ **GO CAMO**
Dress in camouflage colours—neutral tones like tans and dark greens—so you'll look like part of a grassy, bushy or tree-lined landscape. Bright colours can scare away birds. Wear a hat for sun protection, but avoid wearing sunglasses—they make it harder to spot birds. Why? Birds are camouflaged, too!

Timing Is Everything

To spot a specific bird species, you have to time it just right. Songbirds, for instance, have a very predictable pattern: they are lively before dawn in the spring and summer. They wake up hungry and spend their morning eating. When it's hot in the summer and cold in the winter, they often retreat during the afternoon and don't reappear until after sunset. You know what this means: the early bird gets the worm when it comes to looking for songbirds! To spot an owl in flight, you're probably going to have to wait until night, although you might get lucky and spot one roosting during the day.

Shh!

Birds startle very easily. Be quiet and keep your distance so they don't fly away before you've had a chance to get a good look.

Watch Your Step

If you're in a marshy area or at the beach where birds might be nesting on the ground, be careful where you step. And don't disturb a nest if you come across one. If you happen upon a baby bird on the ground, resist the temptation to pick it up. Chances are the mother will be back soon and will tend to it. If you're in doubt about what to do with a bird out of the nest, call your local vet for advice.

Take Notes!

Birding is very hands-on. When you're not looking through binoculars and checking your field guide, you should jot down a few observations you've made. Keep a list of birds you've spotted—or think you've spotted—and then when you go home you can do more research. It's fun to keep a collective list of all the species you've identified. You can also use a notebook or sketch pad to draw a picture of the birds you see. This helps you remember all those details about markings.

Bring the Birds to You

Don't want to travel the world to go birding? Try turning your garden into a bird-friendly habitat. You'll attract certain birds depending on the kind of plants you grow. A garden with tall trees can attract warblers. One with shrubs can lure in Robins and Sparrows. Even a wide-open, manicured lawn can attract birds, like Starlings. Birds also need a reliable water source. Birdbaths with fresh water will attract all kinds of species—even some that aren't attracted to bird feeders.

You can also invite birds to your garden by building a nest box—also known as a birdhouse. The kind of box you build is specific for each species. Search for "nest boxes" on the RSPB website or take a look at what your local garden centre has for sale—you might be able to make something just as good yourself with a little help from a friendly adult.

Turn the page to get started finding and identifying birds!

SHORT STUBBY BILL

BRENT GOOSE

Branta bernicla
LENGTH 56–61cm · **WINGSPAN** 110–120cm
· **WEIGHT** 1.3–1.6kg · **HABITAT** Coastal estuaries
and saltmarshes · **FOOD** Grass and seaweed

A SMALL GOOSE about the size of a large duck. Some have dark and some have pale bellies. They are usually seen around coastal mudflats where they feed mainly on eel grass during the winter. They are winter visitors to the UK, escaping the cold of Russia and Greenland.

VERY SHORT TAIL

WHITE CHINSTRAP

CANADA GOOSE

Branta canadensis
LENGTH 90–110cm · **WINGSPAN** 150–180cm
· **WEIGHT** 4.3–5kg · **HABITAT** Parks and grassy areas
beside lakes and large ponds, often in urban areas
· **FOOD** Grass and seeds, occasionally insects and fish

AS THEIR NAME suggests, these well-known geese originally came from North America but they were introduced into Europe more than 200 years ago. You can see them on lakes and ponds or in fields, but you're more likely to hear them first as they have a distinctive nasal "honk".

LONG BLACK NECK

be a **BIRD NERD**!

In North America where Canada Geese migrate south for the winter, individuals have been known to cover up to 1500 miles (2400km) in 24 hours.

BARRED PLUMAGE

GREYLAG GOOSE

Anser anser
LENGTH 76–89cm · WINGSPAN 147–180cm
· WEIGHT 2.9–3.7kg · HABITAT Wetlands
and estuaries, natural and manmade
· FOOD Grass and leaves

THE GREYLAG IS the largest and bulkiest of the wild geese native to the UK. With its pink legs, a large head and an almost triangular orange-pink bill it's easy to identify. Often found around reservoirs and man-made lakes and ponds, sometimes mixed with Canada Geese.

TRIANGULAR ORANGE-PINK BILL

PINK AND BLACK BILL

PINK-FOOTED GOOSE

Anser brachyrhynchus
LENGTH 60–76cm · WINGSPAN 135–160cm · WEIGHT 2.2–2.7kg
· HABITAT Wetlands and farmland with open water
· FOOD Grain, cereals and root vegetables

A DISTINCTIVE PINK bill as well as the legs and feet of the name make this goose easy to identify. It's one of the bigger birds found in the UK, though not as large as the Greylag Goose. Large numbers winter in the UK before migrating to more northerly latitudes to breed.

PINK FOOT

WHITE-FRONTED GOOSE

Anser albifrons
LENGTH 65–78cm · WINGSPAN 130–165cm
· WEIGHT 1.9–2.5kg · HABITAT Grassland and tidal
wetlands · FOOD Grass, clover and grain

NAMED FOR THE white
patch on the front of their
faces, these medium-sized
geese are relatively rare
winter visitors to the UK
each year.

be a BIRD NERD!

There are two races of White-fronted Goose,
which you can tell apart by the colour of their
bills: Greenland birds have orange bills while
the bills of Siberian birds are pink.

BLACK
BELLY BARS

WHITE FACE

ORANGE BILL

MUTE SWAN

Cygnus olor
LENGTH 140–160cm · WINGSPAN 208–238cm
· WEIGHT 10–12kg · HABITAT Near larger
ponds, small lakes, rivers and canals
all over the country
· FOOD Insects and plants

THIS HUGE BIRD is quite
unmistakable. It has been
said that it is the heaviest
bird capable of flying long
distances. When it does fly
watch it stick out its neck
and use slow deliberate
wingbeats.

BRIGHT
WHITE
PLUMAGE

YELLOW AND BLACK BILL

BEWICK'S SWAN

Cygnus columbianus bewickii
LENGTH 115–127cm · WINGSPAN 170–195cm
· WEIGHT 5.9kg · HABITAT Estuaries and tidal areas
· FOOD Aquatic plants and grass, grain
and root vegetables

A SMALLER SWAN that winters in the UK, it is about half the size of a Mute Swan and has a yellow and black bill. They look very similar to Whooper Swans which also migrate to the UK during winter, but the Whooper Swan is usually larger and has more yellow on its bill.

WHITE PLUMAGE OVER WHOLE BODY

DARK GREEN HEAD

SHELDUCK

Tadorna tadorna
LENGTH 58–65cm · WINGSPAN 110–133cm
· WEIGHT 1–1.4kg · HABITAT Lakes, reservoirs and
coastal areas · FOOD Shellfish

THE BOLD COLOURS of this bird make it easily recognisable even at a distance. It is one of the larger ducks found in the UK and is usually located around coastal estuaries. Look out for the red knob at the base of the male's beak.

RED KNOB AT
BASE OF THE BEAK

MANDARIN

Aix galericulata
LENGTH 40–50cm • **WINGSPAN** 68–74cm
• **WEIGHT** 450–700g • **HABITAT** Shaded ponds with
trees and plants around • **FOOD** Insects and plants

ORIGINALLY FROM CHINA,
large numbers escaped from
private collections of
ornamental wildfowl and
now they adorn our lakes
and slower rivers. The male
especially is particularly
colourful and elaborately
decorated. Unusually for a
duck, it nests in holes in trees.

LONG FACIAL
FEATHERS (MALE)

WHITE STRIPE
BEHIND EYE
(FEMALE)

be a BIRD NERD!

Ducks moult to replace their feathers with
new ones. This process happens in two
stages. The first set of new feathers are
called eclipse feathers and these are
duller than the the more normal feathers
especially on male birds. This gives them
some protection from predators by making
them less noticeable until their new flight
feathers have grown back.

LARGE SPATULATE BILL

SHOVELER

Anas clypeata
LENGTH 44–52cm · WINGSPAN 70–85cm
· WEIGHT 400g–1kg · HABITAT Marshland and small lakes
· FOOD Small insects and water-based plants

AN UNMISTAKABLE DUCK, its wide, flat specialised bill enables it to filter feed on weeds, crustaceans and small insects at the water's edge. It prefers areas of deep cover, and outside of the breeding season, even the drake (male) is actually quite drab. The best place to see a Shoveler would be a nature reserve during winter.

CHESTNUT FLANKS (MALE)

YELLOW FOREHEAD (MALE)

WIGEON

Anas penelope
LENGTH 45–50cm · WINGSPAN 75–85cm
· WEIGHT 500–900g · HABITAT Coastal wetlands
· FOOD Aquatic plants

THESE ARE EASILY located by their unmistakable whistling call. There are not many Wigeons resident all year round, but in winter numbers can reach well into the hundreds of thousands as residents are supplemented by migrants from Russia and the East.

SHORT BILL

GREEN HEAD
(MALE)

MALLARD

Anas platyrhynchos
LENGTH 51–62cm   WINGSPAN 81–99cm
WEIGHT 750g–1.5kg   HABITAT Wetlands, lakes and ponds   FOOD Seeds, berries, insects and shellfish

THE MALLARD IS a common sight around the country's rivers, ponds and lakes and is the bird that people often think of as the typical wild duck. The male is colourful with his green head and purple chest, while the female is predominently light brown.

CURLED TAIL
FEATHERS
(MALE)

PINTAIL

Anas acuta
LENGTH 63–70cm   WINGSPAN 80–95cm
WEIGHT 500g–2kg   HABITAT Sheltered coastal regions and estuaries   FOOD Plants and insects

LARGER THAN A Mallard, its pointed wings and tapering tail make it easy to distinguish from other ducks. It lives in marshy ground while breeding and moves to estuaries during winter to join the many thousands that migrate from Europe.

LONG TAIL
(MALE)

WHITE CHEST
(MALE)

GREEN
EYE PATCH
(MALE)

GREEN
UNDERWINGS

TEAL

Anas crecca
LENGTH 34-39cm · WINGSPAN 58-64cm · WEIGHT 240-360g
· HABITAT Low-lying wetlands · FOOD Seeds and insects

THE TEAL IS the smallest UK resident duck. They are never far from water and nest in thick vegetation beside bogs and pools on northern moorland. During winter they form large flocks and gather to feed on estuaries and adjacent grassland. Males have a brown head with green eye patches.

BROWN HEAD
(MALE)

BLACK BREAST
(MALE)

POCHARD

Aythya ferina
LENGTH 45-48cm · WINGSPAN 75-79cm
· WEIGHT 900-950g · HABITAT Small lakes
and open water bodies · FOOD Plants, seeds,
small insects and molluscs

THE POCHARD IS a striking bird that regularly visits the ponds and lakes in London's Royal Parks. However, outside of the captial its preferred home is flooded gravel pits and other large lakes.

Joke: How did the duck pay for her lipstick?

Answer: She asked to have it added to her bill!

Laugh Out Loud!

TUFTED DUCK

Aythya fuligula
LENGTH 40–47cm · WINGSPAN 67–75cm
· WEIGHT 450–1kg · HABITAT Larger
ponds, small lakes and reservoirs
· FOOD Molluscs and insects

THIS SMALL DIVING duck gets its name from the tuft on its head. The male is a distinctive black and white, while the female is chocolate brown. They can be found in great numbers on lakes, reservoirs and flooded gravel pits.

HEAD TUFT

BLUE-GREY BILL

BLACK AND WHITE BODY WITH A GREEN NAPE (MALE)

MOTTLED BROWN (FEMALE)

EIDER

Somateria mollissima
LENGTH 50–70cm · WINGSPAN 80–110cm
· WEIGHT 1.2–2.8kg · HABITAT Coastal wetlands and estuaries · FOOD Shellfish and molluscs

THE EIDER IS a true seaduck, rarely found inland. They nest on the ground, usually on small islands for safety. Until quite recently, their old down nest-linings were collected, cleaned and used in quilts, though synthetic materials have replaced a lot of this industry. The male is black and white in the breeding season, while the female is mottled brown.

be a BIRD NERD!

The Farne Islands on the Northumberland coast has had a colony for almost 1,500 years!

GOLDENEYE

Bucephala clangula
LENGTH 42–50cm · WINGSPAN 65–80cm
· WEIGHT 650–1.2kg · HABITAT Sheltered wetlands and
coastal regions · FOOD Shellfish, fish and insects

GOLDENEYE SIGHTINGS in winter in this country are getting more common than they used to be partly due to programmes of encouragement and nesting boxes that have been placed in special reserves. They can be found around inland waterways and marshes. Rather unusually for ducks, they nest in trees.

WHITE FACE PATCH
(MALE)

SHAGGY DOUBLE
CREST

RED-BREASTED MERGANSER

Mergus serrator
LENGTH 52–58cm · WINGSPAN 70–85cm
· WEIGHT 900–1.35kg · HABITAT Coastal areas mainly,
but also inland lakes and reservoirs · FOOD Fish

THIS FAIRLY LARGE duck is easily recognised by its spikey head. It can be found all over the country but more typically around coastal regions. It has a serated bill which helps it keep a grip of slippery fish.

LONG THIN ORANGE
BILL (MALE)

BIRDTASTICS:
Arctic Tundra Birds

Arctic Skua

Stercorarius parasiticus
LENGTH: 40–46cm
WINGSPAN: 110–125cm
FOOD: Fish, young birds, eggs and roadkill!

Snow Goose

Anser caerulescens
LENGTH: 65–80cm
WINGSPAN: 130–165cm
FOOD: Grass, vegetation
BE A BIRD NERD: Like many geese it has a distinctive nasal honking call, but you'll be very lucky to hear it as they are pretty rare visitors to the UK.

Arctic Tern

Sterna paradisaea
LENGTH: 33–35cm
WINGSPAN: 75–85cm
FOOD: Fish
BE A BIRD NERD: It migrates from the Arctic to Antarctica, more than 25,000 miles (40,000 km)—the longest migration in the animal kingdom!

THE ARCTIC is the most northerly part of the world, lying between the North Pole and the Arctic Circle. Temperatures, even in summer, rarely rise above 10°C. Trees don't grow in the cold, desert-like Arctic, but there is tundra—flat land where the ground thaws in summer. In May and June, millions of birds migrate there to breed, though some stop off to nest in the UK instead.

BEARD FEATHERS (MALE)

CAPERCAILLIE

Tetrao urogallus
LENGTH 60–87cm · WINGSPAN 85–125cm
· WEIGHT 1.5–5kg
· HABITAT Pine and conifer woodlands
· FOOD Plants and berries

THIS BIRD IS a huge woodland grouse that spends a lot of time looking for food on the ground, but can also be spotted in trees. They live in Scottish native pinewood, which is a rare and vulnerable habitat, and they are in danger of becoming extinct.

COLOURFUL PLUMAGE (MALE)

BLACK GROUSE

Tetrao tetrix · WINGSPAN 65–80cm
LENGTH 40–55cm · WINGSPAN 65–80cm
· WEIGHT 900–1.2kg · HABITAT Sparsely wooded hills and moorland · FOOD Buds, shoots and berries

THE MALE AND FEMALE, both with a distinctive lyre-shaped tail, are often called "Black Cock" and "Grey Hen". They are rare even on their upland moorland habitat, and are very sensitive to disturbance.

BRIGHT RED WATTLES ABOVE THE EYE (MALE)

GLOSSY BLACK PLUMAGE (MALE)

BLACK EYE PATCH

WHITE PLUMAGE [WINTER]

PTARMIGAN

Lagopus muta

LENGTH 34–36cm · WINGSPAN 54–60cm · WEIGHT 400–600g
· HABITAT Lightly covered upland grassland
· FOOD Shoots, leaves, berries and some insects

THE PTARMIGAN IS a grey, brown and black game bird, slightly larger than a grey partridge. These birds breed in the highest mountains of the Highlands of Scotland and rarely leave there, apart from in severe cold weather.

be a BIRD NERD!

In the winter the Ptarmigan becomes completely white, apart from its tail and eyepatch, which remain black.

LIGHTLY HOOK-TIPPED BEAK

REDDISH-BROWN FEATHERS

RED GROUSE

Lagopus lagopus

LENGTH 37–42cm · WINGSPAN 55–65cm
· WEIGHT 650–750g · HABITAT Heather moorlands
· FOOD Heather, insects, seeds and berries

PROBABLY THE MOST famous of this group, the Red Grouse is found on heather moorland, and is unfortunately in decline. When disturbed, these birds fly low with a call which sounds like *go-back-go-back*.

RED-LEGGED PARTRIDGE

Alectoris rufa
LENGTH **32–34cm** · WINGSPAN **47–50cm**
· WEIGHT **400–550g** · HABITAT **Farmland and open grassland** · FOOD **Seeds and roots**

NICKNAMED "FRENCHMEN"
by the shooting fraternity, this type of partridge has been introduced into Britain from mainland Europe. It is slightly larger than our native breed and appears to thrive in farmland bounded by woods.

BOLD, BLACK
FLANK STRIPES

RED LEGS

GREY PARTRIDGE

ORANGE FACE

Perdix perdix
LENGTH **27–30cm** · WINGSPAN **45–48cm**
· WEIGHT **350–420g** · HABITAT **Farmland and lightly wooded grassland** · FOOD **Leaves, seeds and insects**

AN ORANGE-FACED,
plump-breasted game bird that has joined the RSPB Red List due to habitat loss and modern farming methods. It is a sociable bird outside of the breeding season and forms groups called "coveys" for safety.

be a BIRD NERD!

Strictly a ground bird, and therefore not at all likely to be found in a pear tree!

PLUMP, GREY
BREAST

LONG, POINTED WINGS

QUAIL

Coturnix coturnix
LENGTH 15–18cm · **WINGSPAN 30–35cm**
· **WEIGHT 75–135g** · **HABITAT Farmland and open
grassland** · **FOOD Seeds and insects**

THE QUAIL IS a diminutive game bird, which comes to visit us in the late spring and stays until autumn. Rarely seen, it has a distinctive *wet-my-lips* call, and hunts for insects in standing crops. For a ground bird, they have long wings in comparison to their body length.

STOCKY BODY

PHEASANT

WHITE NECK RING (MALE)

Phasianus colchicus
LENGTH 53–89cm · **WINGSPAN 70–90cm**
· **WEIGHT 750–1.7kg** · **HABITAT Open countryside, heathland
and lightly wooded areas** · **FOOD Seeds, grain and insects.**

THE BRIGHTLY COLOURED male Pheasant is unmistakable. These birds are found in most types of country where there are seeds and berries to feed on. The Pheasant is native to Asia but was introduced into the UK a long time ago—there are records of Pheasants going back to before the Norman Conquest!

LONG POINTED TAIL

RED-THROATED DIVER

Gavia stellata
LENGTH 53–69cm · WINGSPAN 105–116cm · WEIGHT 1.2–1.6kg · HABITAT **Primarily coastal waters but also inland lakes** · FOOD **Fish**

THIS IS THE smallest of the UK's diver birds, and is distinguishable by its unusual beak and grey-brown feathers. They jump up out of the water before diving, and can stay underwater for a minute and a half.

RED PLUMAGE ON THE NECK
(SUMMER)

GREAT NORTHERN DIVER

Gavia immer
LENGTH 70–90cm · WINGSPAN 125–150cm · WEIGHT 3.5–4.5kg · HABITAT **Lakes and coastal water regions** · FOOD **Fish and shellfish**

THIS DIVER IS the UK's least common, only generally visiting our shores in the winter. It has a bigger, heavier head than its more common relatives, and eats fish and crustaceans.

LARGE BILL

BLACK AND WHITE SPECKLED PLUMAGE

CHESTNUT-RED THROAT
(SUMMER)

LITTLE GREBE

Tachybaptus ruficollis
LENGTH 25–30cm · WINGSPAN 40–45cm
· WEIGHT 100–150g · HABITAT Sheltered lakes and
coastal regions, with plenty of aquatic plants and
vegetation around · FOOD Insects and small fish

THE LITTLE GREBE is a small and dumpy bird compared to its relatives, and has a bright chestnut throat in the summer. If alarmed they will dive and emerge a fair distance from the perceived danger.

SHORT BODY

ORNATE
HEAD TUFTS

GREAT CRESTED GREBE

Podiceps cristatus
LENGTH 45–50cm · WINGSPAN 85–90cm
· WEIGHT 550–1.5kg
· HABITAT Lowland lakes and ponds, slow
running rivers · FOOD Fish

THIS ATTRACTIVE AND elegant bird dives to feed and also to escape, preferring this to flying. They perform an elaborate courtship routine in which they rise out of the water, shaking their heads. When very young, little grebes are known to take a ride through the water on their parents' backs.

LONG BEAK

LONG, POWERFUL BEAK

BITTERN

Botaurus stellaris
LENGTH 68–80cm · WINGSPAN 100–130cm
· WEIGHT 1–2kg · HABITAT Marshes and wetlands
· FOOD Fish, small reptiles and amphibians

THE BROWN AND black Bittern is a thickset member of the heron family, usually frequenting reedbeds and similar marshy areas, feeding on amphibians, reptiles, insects and fish. The male has a distinctive low-pitched mating call— a far-carrying *boom*.

DARK STREAKS

GREY HERON

Ardea cinerea
LENGTH 90–100cm · WINGSPAN 175–200cm
· WEIGHT 1.5–2kg · HABITAT Anywhere there are
open bodies of water, even beside garden ponds if
they have fish in them! · FOOD Fish mainly, but
also small mammals and amphibians

THE GREY HERON is easy to recognise even in flight. It flies with slow, lazy-looking wing beats and its long legs trail out behind. It is often mobbed by smaller birds. As well as lots of fish, these birds also eat small birds, mammals and amphibians.

LONG LEGS

LONG NECK

GREAT WHITE EGRET

Ardea alba
LENGTH 80–105cm · WINGSPAN 130–175cm
· WEIGHT 700g-1.5kg · HABITAT Grasses and
reedbeds near lakes and open water
· FOOD Fish and amphibians

THIS HERON HAS all-white plumage, and is a similar size to its relative the Grey Heron. It stalks its prey slowly and even waits, motionless, before using its beak to spear its catch when it comes within range.

LONG YELLOW-
ORANGE BILL

LONG NECK

LONG BLACK BEAK

LITTLE EGRET

Egretta garzetta
LENGTH 55–65cm · WINGSPAN 85–95cm
· WEIGHT 350–550g · HABITAT Shores of lakes and
ponds, marshes and reedbeds · FOOD Fish, insects,
small reptiles and amphibians

ONLY 10 YEARS ago it was rare to see a Little Egret. It is now commonly sighted in marshes and rivers, but most often in large numbers at favoured southern coastal sites.

LONG NECK

GANNET

Morus bassanus

LENGTH 87–100cm · WINGSPAN 165–180cm
· WEIGHT 2.4–3.6kg · HABITAT Sea cliffs
around the coast · FOOD Fish

THE GANNET IS our largest seabird with a wingspan of up to 180cm (71 inches)! When these birds dive for fish they fold themselves into an arrow shape—everything is streamlined and designed to pierce the water. They nest in huge numbers on steep cliffs but can often be seen from the shore.

10s spotter

BLACK AND BLUE BEAK

YELLOW HEAD FEATHERS

be a BIRD NERD!

Gannets have a number of special features which allow them to dive and catch fish more efficiently. They have no nostrils to fill with water, but they do have air sacs to cushion their impact. They are so good at catching fish it has led to the term "gannet" being rather unfairly used to describe someone who eats a lot of food.

SHAG

Phalacrocorax aristotelis
LENGTH 65–80cm · WINGSPAN 90–105cm
WEIGHT 1.75–2.25kg · HABITAT Found in coastal areas,
particularly on Scottish islands · FOOD Fish and shellfish

THE SHAG IS a member of the same family as the Cormorant and is very similar to that bird in appearance, but smaller and rarely seen away from the coast. In the spring this bird boasts a shaggy crest on its head which accounts for its name—the Cormorant does not get this crest. The Shag's plumage appears dark green and oily.

SMALL HEAD, PEAKED FOREHAED

DARK GREEN, GLOSSY FEATHERS

YELLOW SKIN AROUND FACE

LONG NECK

CORMORANT

Phalacrocorax carbo
LENGTH 80–100cm · WINGSPAN 130–160cm · WEIGHT 2–2.5kg
· HABITAT Coastal regions, estuaries and lakes · FOOD Fish

DISTINCTIVE-LOOKING BIRDS, Cormorants are regarded by some as greedy, as they are excellent fishers and can find themselves in trouble with anglers. Watch out for them holding out their wings to dry after they have been diving for food.

be a BIRD NERD!

One way to tell a Cormorant from a Shag is to look at the bill and head. The Shag's bill is more slender and the forehead angle is steeper, while the Cormorant has more yellow on its face.

GOLDEN EAGLE

Aquila chrysaetos
LENGTH 75–90cm · WINGSPAN 200–220cm
· WEIGHT 3–6.5kg   HABITAT Open moorland
· FOOD Other birds and small mammals

THIS HUGE BIRD of prey is the second largest found in the UK (after the White-tailed Eagle). It has broad wings with "fingered" tips on which it soars while looking for live prey, like mountain hares and carrion. It is estimated that around 400 pairs live in Scotland, with a few visiting northern England each year looking for new territories to expand into.

be a BIRD NERD!

Eagles are a very popular choice for a country's national animal. Perhaps the most well known is the Bald Eagle of the USA, but more countries, including Albania, Mexico and Kazakhstan, have the Golden Eagle as their national animal.

BROAD WINGS

FEATHERED LEGS

SHORT, HOOKED BEAK

SPARROWHAWK

Accipiter nisus
LENGTH 28–38cm · WINGSPAN 55–70cm
· WEIGHT 100–350g · HABITAT Open country
and woodland, but also urban areas
· FOOD Small birds

A SMALL BIRD of prey, the Sparrowhawk hunts along hedgerows and even in gardens! The male of the species is more colourful but smaller than the female, which is large enough to catch birds such as pigeons. As well as hunting smaller birds, like the Thrush, Sparrowhawks will also look for bats.

BARS ON UNDERSIDE

GOSHAWK

Accipiter gentilis
LENGTH 48–62cm · WINGSPAN 135–165cm
· WEIGHT 600–2kg · HABITAT Light woodland
· FOOD Birds and small mammals

THIS HANDSOME HAWK is around the same size as a Buzzard, but is much more agile. It darts through the trees at high speed while hunting smaller birds, and its long legs and talons allow it to catch prey whilst in flight. It can also soar through the sky to spot mammals on the ground.

WHITE EYEBROWS

LONG LEGS

HEN HARRIER

Circus cyaneus
LENGTH 44–52cm · WINGSPAN 100–120cm · WEIGHT
300–600g · HABITAT Moorland, heathland and farmland
· FOOD Small birds and small mammals

HEN HARRIERS ARE elegant
birds of prey, often found in
the driven grouse moors in
England and Scotland. Here
they glide low in search of
food, which usually consists of
meadow pipits and voles. The
male of this species is the more
beautiful, with pale grey-blue
plumage, whereas females and
younger birds are a mottled brown.

LONG TAIL

LIGHT BELLY

WHITE-TAILED EAGLE

PALE HEAD

Haliaeetus albicilla
LENGTH 70–90cm · WINGSPAN 200–250cm · WEIGHT 3.5–7kg
HABITAT Coastal regions and lightly wooded areas near water
· FOOD Fish, other brids, and mammals.

WHITE TAIL
FEATHERS

WHITE-TAILED EAGLES are the
largest birds of prey in the UK.
Their prey is varied, and includes
smaller birds, rabbits and hares,
but their diet is mostly fish.
When hunting, they often steal
the catches of other birds or even
otters. They will also be seen flying
low over the water, hovering
momentarily before snatching fish
from the surface. The species was
extinct here in the early 20th century,
and our current population is descended
from reintroduced birds.

BUZZARD

Buteo buteo
LENGTH 50–57cm · **WINGSPAN** 113–128cm · **WEIGHT** 550–1.3kg
HABITAT Farmland, scrubland and light woodlands
FOOD Small mammals, small birds and insects

CONSERVATIONISTS HAVE triumphed! Buzzards can once again regularly be seen sitting on a roadside fence post or wheeling over the open countryside. Their numbers had fallen so drastically that at the start of the 20th century there were only around 1,000 breeding pairs. Today there are around 60,000 breeding pairs in the UK and in fact, they are now the most common and widespread birds of prey in the country. Listen for their "mewing" call.

HOOKED YELLOW AND BLACK BEAK

BROWN PLUMAGE

10s spotters

BIRDTASTICS: Comeback Kings

Red Kite

Milvus milvus
LENGTH: 60–65cm
WINGSPAN: 175–195cm
FOOD: Carrion and small mammals like mice and voles
FACT: Brought back from the brink of national extinction in the 1980s.

A SPECIES becomes endangered when there are so few left in the wild that they could disappear altogether. Each of these bird species were hunted so much that they either went extinct in the UK—Great Bustards in 1832, Ospreys in 1916—or got perilously close to it. Red Kites got down to 20 pairs in the 1960s. National or local protection programmes have brought all of these species back from the brink and now their numbers are on the increase in this country again.

AN OSPREY SWOOPS DOWN TO
GRASP A TROUT FROM THE WATER.

Osprey

Pandion haliaetus
LENGTH: 50–60cm
WINGSPAN: 145–170cm
FOOD: Fish
FACT: Ospreys are rare summer visitors
to very specific locations in Scotland,
England and Wales.

Great Bustard

Otis tarda
LENGTH: 115cm
WINGSPAN: 200–270cm
FOOD: Insects, plants and seeds
FACT: The male has very distinctive
beard-like feathers around its beak.

GREY FACE

WATER RAIL

Rallus aquaticus
LENGTH 23–28cm · WINGSPAN 38–45cm
· WEIGHT 80–180g
· HABITAT Coastal lowland regions
· FOOD Small fish and insects

THIS HIGHLY SECRETIVE but fairly common bird is distinctly smaller and slimmer than its Moorhen relative, and can be found (when spotted) in fresh-water wetlands. Although it is more widespread in winter, it is more likely to be heard than seen, at any time of year.

LONG RED BILL

CORNCRAKE

Crex crex
LENGTH 27–30cm · WINGSPAN 46–53cm
· WEIGHT 120–200g · HABITAT Coastal
and marsh areas of Scottish islands
· FOOD Insects and seeds

UNLIKE THEIR Moorhen, Coot and Rail relatives, Corncrakes live on dry land. They do, however, share some traits with these birds in that they are famously secretive and often only betrayed by their rasping call. They have bright chestnut wings and trailing legs, which are unmistakable in flight.

CHESTNUT WINGS

PINKISH-BROWN LEGS

RED AND YELLOW BEAK

MOORHEN

Gallinula chloropus
LENGTH 32-35cm · WINGSPAN 50-55cm · WEIGHT 250-400g
· HABITAT Around ponds and lakes all over the country
· FOOD Water plants, insects and small fish

MOORHENS ARE PERHAPS the most commonly spotted of their family of species, although they too can be quite shy. They live in most kinds of watery areas where plants grow. Their most distinctive feature is the red patch on the front of the head and base of the beak, but look out for a constantly flicking white tail, as well.

LONG, STRAIGHT NECK

WHITE BEAK AND "SHIELD"

COOT

Fulica atra
LENGTH 36-38cm · WINGSPAN 70-80cm
· WEIGHT 600-900g · HABITAT Freshwater lakes
and ponds, in the countryside or in urban areas
· FOOD Seeds, plants and insects

"AS BALD AS A COOT!" or so the saying goes. Coots are not actually bald but they do have a white patch on the forehead and beak. They are found on lakes, flooded gravel pits and reservoirs, where they can be heard pattering noisily over the water before taking off, or even occasionally being aggressive towards other birds!

ALL-BLACK PLUMAGE

CRANE

Grus grus
LENGTH 110–120cm · WINGSPAN 220–245cm
· WEIGHT 4–7kg · HABITAT Shallow wetlands or
grassland close to water · FOOD Seeds, roots,
insects, worms and snails

NOT TO BE confused with
the Heron, the Crane is
another tall bird with a
long neck and legs. Cranes,
however, have shorter
beaks and stick their necks
out straight when flying.
There are small breeding
populations to be found in Norfolk
and Somerset, and additional small
numbers pass through Britain in spring
and autumn.

LONG NECK

DROOPING,
CURVED TAIL
FEATHERS

Laugh Out Loud!

Joke: Which bird is the
best at lifting heavy
weights?

Answer: A Crane!

10s
spotters

LONG, ORANGE-RED BILL

REDDISH-PINK LEGS

OYSTERCATCHER

Haematopus ostralegus
LENGTH 40–45cm · WINGSPAN 80–86cm
WEIGHT 430–650g · HABITAT Coastal reserves and
estuaries · FOOD Mussels, cockles and worms

WITH ITS BRIGHT orange-red
bill, pinkish-red legs, red eyes
and black and white plumage,
the Oystercatcher is easy to
recognise at the coast,
though some are now breeding
inland too. Listen for its loud
piping call.

AVOCET

Recurvirostra avosetta
LENGTH 42–45cm · WINGSPAN 77–80cm
· WEIGHT 260–290g · HABITAT Lagoons and coastal
areas as well as grassland · FOOD Aquatic insects,
invertebrates and worms

THIS BLACK AND WHITE

water wader can be found
searching for aquatic
insects in coastal areas
and grasslands. The
Avocet is also the emblem
of the RSPB, and has
come to symbolise bird
protection, as its return
to the UK and increase in
numbers represents one
of our most successful
conservation and protection
projects.

BLACK AND
WHITE STRIPED
PLUMAGE

LONG, UP-CURVED BEAK

LAPWING

Vanellus vanellus
LENGTH 28–31cm · WINGSPAN 82–87cm
· WEIGHT 140–320g · HABITAT Arable farmland
and low-lying grassland · FOOD Insects and worms

THE LAPWING is a familiar
farmland bird and was given
its name due to its wavering
flight. When moving through
the air, these birds take on a
distinctive round-winged
shape and appear black and
white, as their green upper
bodies are no longer visible.
They can be seen feeding on pasture,
and need undisturbed fields, such as
meadows and set-aside farmland for
nesting.

CREST

DARK GREEN
PLUMAGE

GOLDEN PLOVER

Pluvialis apricaria
LENGTH 26–29cm · WINGSPAN 67–76cm
· WEIGHT 160–280g · HABITAT Moorland and farmland
· FOOD Worms, beetles and insects

THIS IS A medium-sized
plover with an upstanding
posture and amazing gold
and black summer plumage.
In winter they gather in
great numbers and fly about
in formation, with rapid,
flickering wing beats. During
the summer they breed on
moorland but move to lowland fields
to overwinter.

GOLD AND BLACK
PLUMAGE (SUMMER)

BLACK UNDERPARTS

GREY PLOVER

Pluvialis squatarola
LENGTH 28cm · **WINGSPAN** 77cm · **WEIGHT** 240g · **HABITAT** Coastal regions, estuaries and muddy wetlands · **FOOD** Shellfish and worms

LIKE MOST PLOVERS

this bird stands very upright, and may well be spotted running, stopping suddenly to feed. It is generally found in small numbers, though larger groups can form when there is a high tide.

SHORT NECK

LIGHTER WINTER PLUMAGE, DARKER BELLY IN SUMMER

RINGED PLOVER

Charadrius hiaticula
LENGTH 18–20cm · **WINGSPAN** 48–57cm · **WEIGHT** 55–75g · **HABITAT** Beaches, coastal reserves and around reservoirs and lakes · **FOOD** Insects, spiders and molluscs

IN THE WINTER, these

attractive little wading shore birds are found along muddy estuaries. For the rest of the year, they're residents of UK beaches. They are so named because of the black ring around their necks.

ORANGE BEAK WITH BLACK TIP

SHORT LEGS

DOTTEREL

Charadrius morinellus
LENGTH 20–22cm · WINGSPAN 57–65cm
· WEIGHT 90–145g · HABITAT Highlands,
particularly in Scotland · FOOD Worms and insects

THE DOTTEREL is an unusual member of the plover family because the roles during breeding are reversed—the male bird guards the eggs and the female has the brighter plumage. They are often seen in groups known as "trips" during spring migration.

BRIGHT CHESTNUT BELLY

WHITE THROAT AND EYESTRIPE

be a BIRD NERD!

In most of the animal kingdom, females tend to be smaller than males. Most species of birds also follow this trend although there are quite a few bird types where the opposite occurs—females are bigger than the males. This is fairly common in raptors and shorebirds. The Dotterel is one such shorebird species where the female is bigger than the male.

10s spotters

CURLEW

Numenius arquata
LENGTH 50–60cm · WINGSPAN 80–100cm · WEIGHT 500–1kg
· HABITAT Estuaries, coastal wetlands and moorland
· FOOD Worms and shellfish

THIS IS OUR largest wader. It nests on moorland and spends the rest of the year at the coast where it uses its long, curved bill to probe in the mud for worms and shrimps. Its name comes from its *cooer-ieeoo* call.

LONG, DOWN-CURVED BILL

LONG LEGS

BAR-TAILED GODWIT

LONG, SLIGHTLY UP-CURVED BILL

Limosa lapponica
LENGTH 37–39cm · WINGSPAN 70–80cm
· WEIGHT 230–450g · HABITAT Estuaries and tidal areas
· FOOD Shellfish, snails and shrimps

ANOTHER LONG-BILLED wading bird, the Bar-tailed Godwit is usually only found on UK shores during our colder months. These birds breed in the Arctic of Scandinavia and Siberia, and their appearance in the UK occurs as hundreds of thousands of them migrate south, a smaller number stopping off for the winter.

STREAKY BACK

BLACK-TAILED GODWIT

LONG, STRAIGHT BEAK

Limosa limosa
LENGTH 40–44cm · WINGSPAN 70–82cm · WEIGHT 280–340g
· HABITAT Estuaries and tidal marshes, some inland wetlands
· FOOD Insects, snails and some plants

SIMILARLY TO their bar-tailed relatives, these godwits have bright orange-brown chests and bellies in the summer. The females of the species are considerably bigger than the males, with noticeably longer beaks.

LONG LEGS

TURNSTONE

Arenaria interpres
LENGTH 21–24cm · WINGSPAN 50–57cm · WEIGHT 85–150g · HABITAT Rocky shorelines and coastal areas · FOOD Insects and molluscs

TURNSTONES ARE SMALL but sturdy birds, which spend the majority of their time, as their name suggests, scouring rocks and turning over stones in search of their next meal.

SMALL BUT STRONG BILL

BRIGHT ORANGE LEGS

....

KNOT

Calidris canutus
LENGTH 23–25cm · WINGSPAN 47–54cm · WEIGHT 125–215g · HABITAT Estuaries and coastal wetlands · FOOD Shellfish and worms

THE KNOT IS ONE of the shortest, dumpiest wading birds. In summer, the bird's chest, face and belly are a striking brick-red. It forms huge flocks in winter, which twist and turn in flight, flashing pale underwings as they go.

POINTY BEAK

RED CHEST AND BELLY

SANDERLING

Calidris alba
LENGTH 20–21cm · WINGSPAN 36–39cm
· WEIGHT 50–60g · HABITAT Sandy beaches
· FOOD Marine worms and crustaceans

DESPITE BEING SMALL
and plump, the Sanderling
is a most energetic wading
bird. As with many other
species of its kind, it does
not breed in the UK but is
a visitor on its way to and
from its Arctic residence.

STOUT BILL

BLACK LEGS

DUNLIN

Calidris alpina
LENGTH 16–20cm · WINGSPAN 16–20cm
· WEIGHT 40–50g · HABITAT Mudflats
and coastal wetlands · FOOD Insects,
snails, worms and seeds

THE DUNLIN IS the most
common wader found along
the UK's coastline. In
winter, these birds feed in
flocks of up to a thousand
in number, roosting on
nearby saltmarshes, fields and
shore when the tide is high.

DOWN-CURVED
BEAK

BLACK BELLY
(SUMMER)

PURPLE SANDPIPER

Calidris maritima
LENGTH 20–22cm · **WINGSPAN** 20–22cm
· **WEIGHT** 60–75g · **HABITAT** Rocky coastal areas
· **FOOD** Insects, shellfish and some plants

THIS MEDIUM-SIZED wading bird is larger and stockier than its Dunlin cousin, and although it can be seen around the UK coast, it is a relatively rare visitor. There are only a couple of breeding pairs in Scotland, and their whereabouts are kept secret to protect the birds from egg thieves and disturbance.

PLUMP CHEST

BRIGHT ORANGE LEGS

LONG, TAPERING BILL

WOODCOCK

Scolopax rusticola
LENGTH 33–35cm · **WINGSPAN** 55–65cm
· **WEIGHT** 240–420g · **HABITAT** Grassland and
farmland, even some highland areas · **FOOD** Worms,
caterpillars and insect lavae

A WOODCOCK IS a large and bulky wading bird, with a very long, straight, tapering bill. This bird is also nocturnal, spending most of the day in dense cover. Unlike some other waders, most Woodcocks in the UK are residents, although more come from Finland and Russia to winter here.

LARGE BODY

JACK SNIPE

SHORT LEGS

Lymnocryptes minimus
LENGTH 17–19cm · WINGSPAN 38–42cm · WEIGHT 35–70g
· HABITAT Watery lowlands, wetlands, ponds and lakeshores
· FOOD Insects, worms and snails

JACK SNIPES ARE smaller than their close relatives, Snipes. Their mottled plumage allows them to stay well camouflaged in their preferred habitat, which is useful for these secretive birds. When approached, a Jack Snipe is more likely to crouch in an attmept to hide, before flying off.

SLIGHTLY SHORTER BILL THAN A SNIPE

RELATIVELY SMALL BODY

SNIPE

Gallinago gallinago
LENGTH 23–28cm · WINGSPAN 39–45cm
· WEIGHT 80–120g · HABITAT Moorland and wetlands
· FOOD Worms, caterpillars and insect lavae

THIS LONG-BILLED bird is a widespread breeding species in the UK, perhaps best known for its habit of "drumming" during the breeding season. It flies up and then dives with its outer tail feathers spread out to make a throbbing noise.

LONG, STRAIGHT BEAK

POINTY BEAK

COMMON SANDPIPER

Actitis hypoleucos
LENGTH 19–21cm · WINGSPAN 32–35cm · WEIGHT 40–60g
· HABITAT Estuaries and shores of larger water bodies.
Doesn't mind fast flowing water · FOOD Insects and worms

THIS BIRD IS a fairly small, brownish wader, with distinctive behaviours such as "teeter-ing"—which means bobbing up and down—stiff wings in flight, and a recognisable three-note call it gives upon departure.

BROWN PLUMAGE

REDSHANK

Tringa totanus

LENGTH 28cm · WINGSPAN 62cm
· WEIGHT 110–130g · HABITAT Grassland
with access to water and tidal estuaries
· FOOD Insects, worms and molluscs

REDSHANKS WERE GIVEN

their name due to their bright
orange-red legs, which can be
spotted from a distance. They
use their beaks to fish out
insects and earthworms from
mud and soil.

LONG, THIN
BILL

BRIGHT ORANGE-
RED LEGS

BIRDTASTICS:
Open Ocean Birds

Manx Shearwater

Puffinus puffinus
LENGTH: 30–38cm
WINGSPAN: 75–82cm
FOOD: Fish, especially herring,
sardines and sprats.

Leach's Petrel

Oceanodroma leucorhoa
LENGTH: 19–22cm
WINGSPAN: 45–48cm
FOOD: Crustaceans, molluscs and
small fish
BE A BIRD NERD: Tell it apart from
the Storm Petrel by its distinctive
forked tail feathers.

A MANX SHEARWATER GLIDES ON THE WIND.
THEY FLY BY A COMBINATION OF STIFF-WINGED FLAPS
INTERSPERSED WITH LONGER GLIDING PERIODS.

Storm Petrel

Hydrobates pelagicus
LENGTH: 14–18cm
WINGSPAN: 36–39cm
FOOD: Fish and shellfish
BE A BIRD NERD: The typical lifespan of a Storm Petrel is around 10–12 years, but some have been recorded at over 30 years old.

Fulmar

Fulmarus glacialis
LENGTH: 45–50cm
WINGSPAN: 100–115cm
FOOD: Fish waste, sand eels and crustaceans
BE A BIRD NERD: When their nests are threatened they can use their mouths to spray foul-smelling oil at intruders.

SOME BIRDS are at home when they are over the oceans. They are built to fly and can be clumsy on dry land making them vulnerable to predators. For this reason they usually nest on cliffs and rocks where they are only at risk from other birds like skuas and large gulls. The petrels feed by flying close to the water and scooping up fish and squid from just below the surface.

KITTIWAKE

Rissa tridactyla
LENGTH 38–40cm · WINGSPAN 95–110cm
· WEIGHT 300–500g
· HABITAT Mostly at sea but roosts on the coast
· FOOD Fish, sand eels, shrimps and worms

THIS MEDIUM-SIZED gull is noted for its black wing-tips, which look as though they have been dipped in ink. It is a strictly coastal gull and spends the winter months out at sea. Its name is supposedly imitative of the bird's cry.

BLACK WING-TIPS

HOOKED YELLOW BEAK

BLACK-HEADED GULL

DEEP-BROWN HEAD PLUMAGE (SUMMER)

Chroicocephalus ridibundus
LENGTH 34–37cm · WINGSPAN 100–110cm
· WEIGHT 200–400g · HABITAT Found all around the country, inland and near the sea · FOOD Worms, insects, fish and carrion

THESE COMMON GULLS are not only seen at the coast. During the winter, they can be found in most areas. They are sociable and noisy, and often found in groups, so you are unlikely to miss them!

be a BIRD NERD!

The Black-headed Gull's name is pretty misleading as in the summer its head is more brown than black and in the winter it goes almost white!

ORANGE-RED BEAK AND LEGS

MEDITERRANEAN GULL

BLACK HEAD PLUMAGE

LARGE, DROOPED, RED BEAK

Larus melanocephalus
LENGTH 36–38cm · WINGSPAN 90–100cm · WEIGHT 230–280g · HABITAT Coastal areas all around the country · FOOD Insects, fish and carrion

THIS GULL IS slightly larger than its "black-headed" relative and, perhaps confusingly, has more of a black head! It was very rare in the UK until the 1950s, since when it has grown in number to become positively widespread in winter.

COMMON GULL

POINTED YELLOW BEAK

GREENISH LEGS

Larus canus
LENGTH 40–42cm · WINGSPAN 110–130cm · WEIGHT 300–500g · HABITAT Eastern coasts, inland wetlands and lake shores, but will also appear in urban areas if there is food · FOOD Worms, insects, fish and rubbish

A SMALLER VERSION of the Herring Gull, it is abundant in coastal regions and in some eastern counties. Here, they are often seen in towns and on housing estates in winter. Despite its name, however, this bird isn't at all common in most inland areas.

GREAT BLACK-BACKED GULL

POWERFUL, CHUNKY BEAK

BLACK WINGS

Larus marinus
LENGTH 64–78cm · WINGSPAN 150–165cm · WEIGHT 1–2kg · HABITAT Coastal regions, harbours, bays and places where food can be scavenged, like rubbish tips and dumps · FOOD Shellfish, small birds, carrion and rubbish.

THE GREAT BLACK-BACKED Gull is even bigger and more powerful than the Herring Gull. It will attack other birds, especially their chicks in the breeding season. Usually a solitary bird, it may also be seen in mixed gull flocks.

HERRING GULL

Larus argentatus
LENGTH 54–60cm · WINGSPAN 130–150cm
· WEIGHT 690g–1.5kg · HABITAT Anywhere there is
food from coastal estuaries to urban rubbish tips
· FOOD Human food srcraps, carrion, fruit, small
animals like birds and mammals, insects and fish

THE HERRING GULL is a
large, heavily built bird
with pink legs and a yellow
beak bearing a bright red
spot on the underside. It is
found mainly in coastal
regions, but also on rubbish
tips.

CHUNKY BEAK
WITH RED
SPOT

BLACK
WINGS

LESSER BLACK-BACKED GULL

Larus fuscus
LENGTH 52–64cm · WINGSPAN 135–150cm
· WEIGHT 620g–1kg · HABITAT Coastal regions and places
where food can be scavenged · FOOD Shellfish, small
birds, carrion and human rubbish

SLIGHTLY SMALLER THAN
a Herring Gull, this bird
can only be found in
Europe, with 40 per cent
of its numbers being
resident in the UK. More
than half of that UK
population is concentrated
into fewer than ten sites,
where it scavenges for a wide
range of food.

YELLOW LEGS

YELLOW BILL WITH
RED SPOT

SHAGGY CREST

10s spotters

LONG, BLACK BEAK WITH YELLOW TIP

SANDWICH TERN

Sterna sandvicensis
LENGTH 36–41cm · WINGSPAN 95–105cm
· WEIGHT 210–260g · HABITAT Freshwater lakes
and coastal lagoons · FOOD Fish

THIS BIRD IS a very white tern with a black cap on its head and black legs. Many of the important colonies of Sandwich Terns in the UK are able to survive because they are given protection by being located in nature reserves.

COMMON TERN

Sterna hirundo
LENGTH 31–35cm · WINGSPAN 77–98cm
· WEIGHT 90–150g · HABITAT Rocky island shores,
inland lakes and reservoirs · FOOD Fish

NICKNAMED THE "sea swallow" due to its long tail, this graceful bird frequently hovers over water before plunging down for a fish. This type of tern is the most likely to be spotted inland.

RED BEAK WITH BLACKISH TIP

10s spotters

RED LEGS

be a BIRD NERD!

The Common Tern is hard to tell apart from the Arctic Tern and usually spotters have to take an educated guess on which species they are looking at based on the location where the birds are seen.

GUILLEMOT

STRAIGHT BEAK

VERY DARK BROWN PLUMAGE

Uria aalge
LENGTH **38–45cm** · WINGSPAN **64–73cm** · WEIGHT **850g–1.1kg**
· HABITAT **Mostly at sea but nests on rocky coastal cliffs**
· FOOD **Fish and crustaceans**

THESE BIRDS ARE one of the most numerous in the mixed sea bird breeding colonies around the coast of the UK. When not nesting on the bare sea cliff ledges, they spend their lives at sea, where they are sadly vulnerable to oil spills. They are fast fliers and good swimmers.

SHORT NECK

THICK, BLACK BEAK

RAZORBILL

Alca torda
LENGTH **37–39cm** · WINGSPAN **63–67cm**
· WEIGHT **590–730g** · HABITAT **Rocky shores especially around Scotland**
· FOOD **Fish, especially sandeels**

THE LARGEST COLONIES of Razorbills are found in northern Scotland, but they do breed in other parts of the UK. It is not always easy to tell Guillemots and Razorbills apart unless they are in mixed colonies, when this bird looks blacker and rather bigger than the Guillemot.

BLACK PLUMAGE WITH
WHITE PATCH ON WINGS
(SUMMER)

BLACK GUILLEMOT

Cepphus grylle
LENGTH 30–32cm · WINGSPAN 52–58cm
· WEIGHT 300–450g · HABITAT Rocky shores especially
around Scotland · FOOD Fish and crustaceans

THIS LITTLE AUK is typically
found in and around the
larger sea lochs of western
Scotland and the Northern
and Western Isles, but also in
Northern Ireland, the Isle of
Man, and a handful of spots in
England and Wales. Its
bright red legs and feet help
distinguish it from its relatives.

BRIGHT RED FEET

BLACK AND
WHITE BODY

PUFFIN

Fratercula arctica
LENGTH 26–29cm · WINGSPAN 47–63cm
· WEIGHT 320–480g · HABITAT Large colonies on
remote coasts · FOOD Fish, especially sandeels

THE PUFFIN HAS a very
distinctive, almost comical,
look and is widely recognised.
In March they arrive at their
traditional breeding sites on
the coast where they nest in
tunnels. They leave in August to
spend the winter far out to sea.

COLOURFUL
BEAK AND
ORANGE-RED
FEET

be a BIRD NERD!

The Puffin can hold more than 10 fish in its
mouth at once.

ROCK DOVE

Columba livia
LENGTH 31–34cm · WINGSPAN 63–70cm
WEIGHT 230–370g · HABITAT Coastal
regions · FOOD Seeds and cereals

THIS BIRD IS the wild ancestor of the domestic pigeon, and was originally domesticated to provide food. The wild Rock Dove can be found on the coasts of Scotland and Northern Ireland, but the domestic pigeon breeds across the UK and is often considered a pest, particularly in urban areas where numbers are not managed.

PINKY-PURPLE OR GREEN NECK MARKINGS

BLUISH-GREY PLUMAGE

10s spotters

Joke: Why did they put lions in Trafalgar Square?

Answer: They wanted to put the cats amongst the pigeons!

Laugh Out Loud!

GREEN BAND

STOCK DOVE

Columba oenas
LENGTH 30–33cm · WINGSPAN 60–66cm · WEIGHT 290–330g
HABITAT Range of habitats including farmland,
marshland and urban areas · FOOD Seeds

STOCK DOVES ARE found in farmland, parks, the edges of woods, cliffs, ruined buildings and even among sand dunes. Unlike Woodpigeons they nest in holes and feed mainly on seeds. Over half of their European population is found in the UK.

BLUISH-GREY PLUMAGE

WHITE NECK PATCH

WOODPIGEON

Columba palumbus
LENGTH 40–42cm · WINGSPAN 75–80cm · WEIGHT 480–550g
HABITAT Farmland, light woodland, parks and gardens
FOOD Shoots, seeds, fruits and nuts

WHEN WOODPIGEONS TAKE off, they usually make a loud clapping noise with their wings as they strike together. This is thought to help them make a fast getaway. Their familiar cooing call also helps distinguish them from relatives such as the Rock or Stock Dove.

WHITE PATCH ON WING

TURTLE DOVE

Streptopelia turtur
LENGTH 26–28cm
WINGSPAN 47–53cm
WEIGHT 130–180g
HABITAT Grassland, healthland and farmland all over the country
FOOD Seeds and grain

YOU MAY ONLY have heard of this dove because of a popular seasonal song, particularly as it is becoming increasingly rare in the UK! It is a dainty bird, which is more often heard than seen, with the pleasant purring sound it makes.

RED LEGS

MOTTLED PLUMAGE

BLACK COLLAR

COLLARED DOVE

Streptopelia decaocto
LENGTH 32cm · WINGSPAN 51cm · WEIGHT 200g
HABITAT Farmland, parks and gardens
FOOD Seeds and grain

WITH THEIR PINKISH, fawnish, grey colour and black, collar-like mark on either side of the neck, these birds are aptly-named and easy to recognise. They can often be seen in gardens.

PALE PINKY-BROWN PLUMAGE

CUCKOO

Cuculus canorus
LENGTH **32–34cm** · WINGSPAN **55–65cm**
· WEIGHT **105–130g** · HABITAT **Forests,
wooded parks and gardens**
· FOOD **Insects**

THE CUCKOO LOOKS
similar to birds of
prey such as the
Kestrel and the
Sparrowhawk,
particularly when in
flight. These birds are
best known for their habit
of laying their eggs in the
nests of others, giving them a
reputation as "brood parasites".

LONG TAIL

POINTED WINGS

be a BIRD NERD!

While it is usually considered that a Cuckoo in the nest is
a bad thing for the host species, it might not always be the
case. Scientists at the University of Oviedo in Spain found
that crows nests that contained Cuckoo chicks produced
more crows that survived to adulthood. This was because
the Cuckoo chicks were better at defending the nest from
predators than crow chicks were.

EYES RIMMED WITH
DARK FEATHERS

TAWNY OWL

Strix aluco
LENGTH 37–39cm · WINGSPAN 94–105cm
· WEIGHT 330–600g · HABITAT Forests,
wooded parks, gardens and farmland
· FOOD Small mammals, birds,
amphibians and insects

THIS OWL IS a
widespread breeding
species in England,
Wales and Scotland
but is not found in
Ireland. It is the Tawny
Owl that makes the hooting
noise that is commonly
associated with owls. If you
see mobs of small birds seemingly
attacking an ivy-covered tree,
there may well be a Tawny Owl
roosting there.

ROUNDED
HEAD

LITTLE OWL

SMALLER
HEAD

Athene noctua
LENGTH 21–23cm · WINGSPAN 54–58cm
· WEIGHT 140–220g · HABITAT Grassland and
farmland with trees and woods · FOOD Small
mammals, birds and insects

UNLIKE THEIR nocturnal
relatives, Little Owls may
be seen during the day
sitting on a fence post
looking for insects. They
were introduced into the UK
in the late 1800s but their
numbers are now in decline.

MOTTLED BROWN
PLUMAGE

EAR TUFTS

LONG-EARED OWL

Asio otus

LENGTH 35–37cm   WINGSPAN 84–95cm
WEIGHT 210–370g   HABITAT **Forests and wooded grassland**   FOOD **Small birds and rodents**

THIS MEDIUM-SIZED owl is nocturnal and very secretive. It sweeps over the ground in a zig-zag pattern looking for prey.

be a BIRD NERD!

The "ear tufts" are not ears at all, but are raised in alarm to make the owl look bigger when it is under threat.

DEEP ORANGE EYES

....

SHORT-EARED OWL

SMALL EAR TUFTS

Asio flammeus

LENGTH 34–42cm   WINGSPAN 90–105cm
WEIGHT 260–350g   HABITAT **Coastal wetlands and marshland with trees**
FOOD **Small mammals**

SHORT-EARED OWLS are fairly similar to their long-eared cousins, and are often seen hunting during the day. Their UK numbers increase significantly in winter, when more birds migrate from places like Russia, Scandinavia and Iceland.

MOTTLED BROWN PLUMAGE

BIRDTASTICS:
Up All Night

Nightjar

Caprimulgus europaeus
LENGTH: 26–28cm
WINGSPAN: 57–64cm
FOOD: Insects
BE A BIRD NERD:
Camouflaged plumage and silent flight make the Nightjar an excellent night hunter.

Stone Curlew

Burhinus oedicnemus
LENGTH: 40–45cm
WINGSPAN: 77–85cm
FOOD: Ground insects
BE A BID NERD: This ungainly looking bird is not actually related to the Eurasian or Common Curlew at all.

Barn Owl

Tyto alba
LENGTH: 33–39cm
WINGSPAN: 80–95cm
FOOD: Rodents, small to medium-
sized mammals and small birds
BE A BIRD NERD: They do not hoot
like many owls but screech and
hiss instead.

MANY BIRDS hunt both during the day and at night, but several species are much more suited to nocturnal living. Usually they have evolved in a way that helps them find food when others would struggle—Barn Owls for example, have incredibly accurate hearing, whereas Nightjars can fly almost silently. The Stone Curlew has large yellow eyes that allow it to see its food in the dark.

SWIFT

Apus apus

LENGTH 16–17cm   WINGSPAN 42–48cm
WEIGHT 35–50g   HABITAT Farmland
and grassland, nesting in buildings,
hollows and caves   FOOD Flying insects

IT IS FAIRLY easy to spot Swifts, with their long, sickle-shaped wings and fast, agile flight. They also love to swoop in and around old buildings, so you might catch sight of one flying around a ruined countryside barn at breakneck speed. You'll be unlikely to see its nest as Swifts don't build them in the open, preferring holes or hidden spaces, but you probably will hear its shrill scream. While they do nest to breed and raise young, Swifts have been known to stay in the air for more than 100 days without landing. They feed, and even sleep, as they fly!

LONG WINGS

The scientific family name for Swifts, Apodidae, comes from the Greek word for footless. This is because Swifts have very small little legs and it may be that early birdwatchers didn't think they had any legs at all.

SHORT, FORKED TAIL

KINGFISHER

Alcedo atthis

LENGTH 16–17cm **WINGSPAN** 24–26cm **WEIGHT** 34-46g
HABITAT Wetlands, farmland with water bodies, around ponds and smaller lakes **FOOD** Fish and aquatic insects

THE KINGFISHER IS colourful and instantly recognisable. These birds live by still or slow-moving water, where they can be seen perching and waiting for a catch. When hunting, they fly at a fast pace, low over the surface of the water, but they also occasionally hover to pick out their prey.

LONG BEAK

be a BIRD NERD!

Kingfishers have specially adapted eyes for diving into the water to catch their prey. Their vision is not as clear underwater as it is in the air, but they are able to judge distances more accurately and this makes catching fish easier!

COLOURFUL PLUMAGE

10s spotters

LESSER SPOTTED WOODPECKER

Dendrocopos minor
LENGTH 14–15cm · WINGSPAN 25–27cm · WEIGHT 17–25g · HABITAT Woodlands · FOOD Insects

SIMILARLY TO THE Great Spotted Woodpecker, the male bird of this smaller version has a red cap. Its drumming song is quieter and more rapid than that of its larger cousin. It is also the least common of the UK's resident woodpeckers.

RED CAP (MALE)

BLACK AND WHITE STRIPES

CREAM THROAT AND CHEST

GREAT SPOTTED WOODPECKER

Dendrocopos major
LENGTH 22–23cm · WINGSPAN 34–39cm · WEIGHT 85g · HABITAT Woods, parks and gardens · FOOD Insects

THIS BLACK AND WHITE woodpecker has a red patch beneath its tail. It "sings" by drumming its beak against a trunk or branch of a tree. The bird feeds on insects which it digs out from under the bark.

RED PATCH BENEATH THE TAIL

GREEN WOODPECKER

Picus viridis
LENGTH 22–23cm · WINGSPAN 34–39cm · WEIGHT 85g
HABITAT Woods and trees in parks and gardens
· FOOD Insects, especially ants

THE LARGEST OF the woodpeckers to be found in the UK, the Green Woodpecker rarely drums and can often be seen digging for ants on the ground. As its name suggests this bird is predominently green, with male and female birds sporting dark green wings on a pale light green body.

RED CAP

GREEN UPPER PARTS

10s. spotters

Laugh Out Loud!

Joke: What is a woodpecker's favourite type of joke?

Answer: A knock-knock joke!

KESTREL

Falco tinnunculus
LENGTH **32–35cm** · WINGSPAN **71–80cm** · WEIGHT **150–250g** · HABITAT **Open grassland and heathland, countryside and urban areas** · FOOD **Small mammals, birds and insects**

IT IS EASY to see why this bird of prey gets its country name of "windhover". Look out for it hovering by roads and motorways searching for insects and small mammals to pounce on.

GREY HEAD PLUMAGE

SHORT, HOOKED BEAK

MERLIN

Falco columbarius
LENGTH **25–30cm** · WINGSPAN **50–62cm** · WEIGHT **125–300g** · HABITAT **Moorland and open grassland** · FOOD **Small birds**

THE MERLIN IS perhaps most likely to be seen during the winter, frequenting our coastal grasslands where it preys on winter migrants. It hunts down small moorland birds like larks and pipits, which it spots from shrubs, stunted trees, and sometimes fenceposts. This falcon is smaller and faster than a Kestrel.

BLUISH-BLACK PLUMAGE ON UPPER BODY

MOTTLED BROWN UNDERSIDE

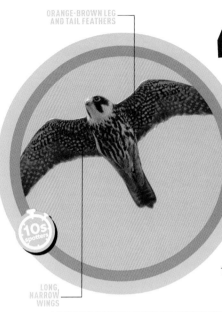

ORANGE-BROWN LEG AND TAIL FEATHERS

LONG, NARROW WINGS

LARGE YELLOW BEAK WITH DARK GREY OR BLACK TIP

LARGE FEET WITH SHARP TALONS

HOBBY

Falco subbuteo
LENGTH 28–36cm · WINGSPAN 70–90cm
· WEIGHT 130-340g · HABITAT Farmland, heathland and open grassland · FOOD Small birds and insects

THIS BIRD OF prey is around the same size as a Kestrel, and is fairly magnificent in flight. It dashes and darts, chasing smaller birds and large insects. It will often grasp its catch with its talons initially, and transfer it to its beak whilst gliding through the air.

PEREGRINE

Falco peregrinus
LENGTH 39–50cm · WINGSPAN 95-115cm · WEIGHT 600g-1.3kg
· HABITAT Marshland and coastal wetlands · FOOD Medium-sized birds including ducks and pigeons

THIS FAST-FLYING, anchor-shaped falcon feeds mainly on birds such as pigeons and doves, which it catches in flight. When it swoops down on its victim it becomes the fastest creature in the world!

be a BIRD NERD!

The "stoop" or dive of the Peregrine can achieve a speed of over 200mph. It is travelling so fast that the Peregrine purposely aims to the side of its victim as a direct hit at that speed could damage the falcon almost as much as its prey.

RING-NECKED PARAKEET

Psittacula krameri

LENGTH 38–42cm · WINGSPAN 42–48cm
WEIGHT 96–139g
HABITAT Urban and suburban woodland
FOOD Fruit, berries and seeds

THIS NOISY BIRD is the UK's only naturalised parrot species. They were introduced to southeast England in the early 1970s and have now increased to many thousands thanks to abundant bird table offerings and garden fruit.

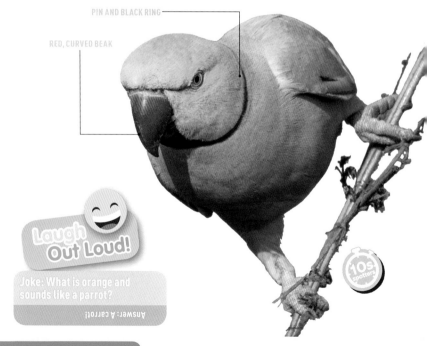

PIN AND BLACK RING

RED, CURVED BEAK

Laugh Out Loud!

Joke: What is orange and sounds like a parrot?

Answer: A carrot!

JAY

Garrulus glandarius
LENGTH 34–35cm · WINGSPAN 52–58cm · WEIGHT 140–190g
· HABITAT Woodland, parks and larger gardens with trees
· FOOD Acorns, nuts, seeds and insects

THIS BRIGHTLY COLOURED member of the crow family is usually a shy bird and you are lucky if you see one flying between patches of woodland. They like to feed on acorns, and will often bury them to retrieve later in the winter.

PINK LEGS

BLUE AND BLACK PATTERNED WING EDGE

IRIDESCENT PLUMAGE

MAGPIE

Pica pica
LENGTH 44–46cm · WINGSPAN 52–60cm · WEIGHT 200–250g
· HABITAT Full range of habitats both urban and countryside · FOOD Omnivorous

VERY COMMON ON our islands, there is no other bird quite like the Magpie in the UK. They are versatile creatures— scavengers, predators and pest detroyers. With their distinctive black and white colouring, they can often be seen at the roadside feeding on roadkill.

LONG TAIL

JACKDAW

Corvus monedula
LENGTH 34cm · WINGSPAN 70cm
· WEIGHT 220g · HABITAT Full range of habitats both urban and countryside · FOOD Insects, young birds, eggs, seeds and scraps

THE JACKDAW IS an untidy-looking bird, smaller than a Rook or a Crow and with a greyish head. This makes it quite easy to identify. Its harsh *tchack* call is also very noticeable.

be a BIRD NERD!

A flock of Jackdaws is called a "Clattering".

GREYISH HEAD

PEAKED HEAD AND BEAK WITH GREY BASE

ROOK

Corvus frugilegus
LENGTH 44–46cm · WINGSPAN 81–99cm · WEIGHT 280–340g
· HABITAT Open grassland and farmland, occasionally in urban areas
· FOOD Small mammals, small birds, insects, seeds and grain

ROOKS ARE OFTEN found in large flocks, feeding on open farmland or in parks and gardens. They are large, glossy black birds, with long beaks that are grey at the base.

STOUT BEAK

CARRION CROW

Corvus corone
LENGTH 45–47cm · WINGSPAN 93–104cm · WEIGHT 370–650g
· HABITAT Found in all areas, urban and countryside
· FOOD Insects, worms, seeds, carrion and scraps

THIS CLEVER MEMBER of the crow family is completely black, including its stout beak that can be used to carry large objects. Although wary, it is actually quite fearless, visiting and returning to gardens and busy areas when it has learnt the coast is clear.

BLACK FACE AND BEAK

GREY BELLY

HOODED CROW

Corvus cornix
LENGTH 45–47cm · WINGSPAN 93–104cm · WEIGHT 370–650g · HABITAT Wetlands and coastal regions, urban and countryside areas of Western Scotland and Northern Ireland · FOOD Insects, worms, seeds, small birds, carrion and scraps

UNLIKE CARRION CROWS
"hoodies" are sociable and often gather in flocks. They have adapted to a harsh life and are omnivorous, feeding on carrion when it's available. Sometimes these crows breed with Carrion Crows and make hybrid birds, with mixed black and grey body plumage.

RAVEN

HEAVY BEAK, BIGGER THAN MOST CROWS

Corvus corax
LENGTH 60–68cm · WINGSPAN 120–150cm · WEIGHT 800g-1.5kg · HABITAT Upland moors and remote countryside areas · FOOD Birds, eggs, small mammals, insects, invertebrates and carrion

THE RAVEN IS completely black with a large beak and a diamond-shaped tail. It is the largest member of the crow family, and is even bigger than a Buzzard!

SHAGGY THROAT FEATHERS

Laugh Out Loud!

Joke: What is a crow's favourite game?

Answer: Croquet!

WAXWING

Bombycilla garrulus
LENGTH 18cm · **WINGSPAN** 32–35cm
· **WEIGHT** 45–70g · **HABITAT** Farmland, eastern
coastal gardens · **FOOD** Berries

THE WAXWING IS a small, plump bird that visits the UK when winter food supplies dwindle in its regular home territory of Scandinavia. It comes here for berries and fruit such as hawthorn and rowan. With its fawny-brown chest, black throat and eye-patch, white and yellow tipped wings and most noticeably its crest, the Waxwing is a very distinctive and easy to recognise bird.

PROMINENT CREST

be a BIRD NERD!

Many birds will travel a long way for food. The Waxwing doesn't breed in the UK and only comes to this country when its Scandinavian winter food source is not sufficient to support the local bird population. For this reason the number of Waxwings seen in the UK varies greatly from year to year, some winters there are only a handful, while thousands make the journey in other years. Aberdeen has seen the highest number of Waxwing sightings in this country. This is because Aberdeen is at the closest point of Great Britain to Norway and so is the first part of land the birds encounter when they travel here over the North Sea.

YELLOW-TIPPED TAIL

COAL TIT

BLACK CAP WITH WHITE PATCH

Periparus ater
LENGTH 11.5cm · WINGSPAN 17–20cm · WEIGHT 8–10g
· HABITAT Heathland and woodland · FOOD Seeds, nuts and insects

ALTHOUGH LESS COLOURFUL than its relatives, the Coal Tit has a smaller beak which means it can feed more successfully in conifer trees. In winter, these birds join mixed-species flocks to visit bird tables and feeders, often storing food they've collected for later.

SMALL, SLENDER BEAK

"BRIDLED" FACE PATTERN

CRESTED TIT

Lophophanes cristatus
LENGTH 11.5cm · WINGSPAN 17–20cm
· WEIGHT 10–13g · HABITAT Pine forests in Scotland · FOOD Seeds and insects

THIS DISTINCITVE-LOOKING tit is less common than most of its relatives in the UK. It feeds actively, clinging to trunks and hanging from branches looking for food that it will often store.

BLACK AND WHITE CREST

MARSH TIT

NO PALE WING PANEL

Poecile palustris
LENGTH 11.5cm · WINGSPAN 18–20cm · WEIGHT 10–13g
· HABITAT Forests, hedges, parks and gardens · FOOD Seeds and insects

THE MARSH TIT and Willow Tit look so similar with their black caps, dark bibs and pale bellies, that ornithologists didn't realise they were two separate species until 1897! The best way to tell them apart is by their call. The Marsh Tit has a quick, sneeze-like *pitchou* call, while the Willow Tit makes a *chay-chay* sound.

DARK BIB

BLACK CAP

WILLOW TIT

Poecile montanus
LENGTH 11.5cm · **WINGSPAN** 17–19cm · **WEIGHT** 8–14g
· **HABITAT** Marshes, wetlands and willow hedges
· **FOOD** Insects, berries and seeds

THIS SPECIES OF tit is much less common than others, and now a Red List bird due to its recent population decline. This bird is incredibly similar to the Marsh Tit but, despite their slightly misleading names, it is the Willow Tit that prefers to be near water.

PALE WING PANEL

BLUE CAP

BLUE TIT

Cyanistes caeruleus
LENGTH 12cm · **WINGSPAN** 18cm · **WEIGHT** 11g
HABITAT Light woodland, gardens and parks
FOOD Insects, seeds, nuts, garden table scraps

THESE LITTLE BIRDS are common visitors to UK gardens, where they are very welcome, given that they eat more aphids (small, plant-eating insects) than any other species. They are well-known for their acrobatics at bird feeders.

YELLOW BELLY

GREAT TIT

Parus major
LENGTH 14cm · WINGSPAN 24cm · WEIGHT 18g
HABITAT Woodland, parks and gardens
FOOD Insects, seeds and nuts

THE LARGEST OF the UK's tits, this bird's blue-black head, white cheek patches, and yellow breast with a black bar down the centre make it easily identifiable. The male's *teacher-teacher* song is also a familiar spring sound.

BLACK BREAST MARKINGS

WHITE CHEEK PATCHES

BLACK "MOUSTACHE" (MALE)

BEARDED TIT

Panurus biarmicus
LENGTH 12.5cm · WINGSPAN 16–18cm · WEIGHT 12–18g
HABITAT Wetlands and reedbeds · FOOD Insects and seeds

IN SPITE OF their name, the males of this species in fact have black markings more like moustaches than beards. These birds are sociable and noisy, with a *ping* call. Bearded Tits are always found around water as their alternative name "Bearded Reedling" suggests.

be a BIRD NERD!

It was named back in the 18th century, but the Bearded Tit is actually quite a unique bird and isn't a member of the tit family at all. The Bearded Tit's closest relatives are now thought to be the larks.

LONG TAIL

WOODLARK

Lullula arborea
LENGTH **15cm** · WINGSPAN **27–30cm** · WEIGHT **25–35g**
· HABITAT **Heathland and woodland**
· FOOD **Seeds and insects**

AS WITH MOST birds in the lark family, the Woodlark is primarily vegetarian as an adult, although it will occasionally eat insects during the breeding season. It is a mottled brown bird easily confused with the Tree Pipit.

WHITE EYE-STRIPE THAT
MEETS ACROSS THE NAPE

MOTTLED PATTERN
OVER MOST OF BIRD
INCLUDING HEAD

SKYLARK

Alauda arvensis
LENGTH **18–19cm** · WINGSPAN **30–36cm**
· WEIGHT **33–45g** · HABITAT **Moorland, farmland and wetlands** · FOOD **Seeds and insects**

SKYLARKS HAVE A tuneful, high-pitched and fast-paced call, and are also known for their display flights, in which they rise from the ground singing, reaching heights of 300m. They are also widely written about in poetry.

CREST

WHITE-SIDED
TAIL

SAND MARTIN

Riparia riparia
LENGTH 12cm · WINGSPAN 26–29cm · WEIGHT 13–14g
· HABITAT Along rivers and beside other
water bodies · FOOD Flying insects

THIS BIRD IS similar to a House
Martin in appearance, but has brown
plumage above and on its wings, and a
white underside with a brown bar across
its chest. The name makes referrence to
the nesting habits of this species, which
chooses burrows in sandy cliffs as its home.

BAR ON
CHEST

SHORT,
FORKED
TAIL

RED THROAT

SWALLOW

Hirundo rustica
LENGTH 17–19cm · WINGSPAN 32–35cm · WEIGHT 16–25g · HABITAT Farmland
with water around, wetlands and reedbeds · FOOD Flying insects

FAMILIAR BIRDS OF summer, Swallows are
very graceful in flight and feed by catching
insects as they go. They will also swoop
down over lakes and rivers to drink. Look
out for their long tail streamers.

HOUSE MARTIN

GLOSSY,
BLUISH-BLACK
UPPERPARTS

Delichon urbicum
LENGTH 12cm · WINGSPAN 26–29cm · WEIGHT 15–23g
· HABITAT Farmland and woodland, near water
Sometimes in semi-urban areas · FOOD Insects

THIS BIRD SPENDS much of its time in
the air, and usually nests below the eaves
of buildings. It is the white bar at the base
of the tail which will allow you to distinguish
House Martins from Swallows or Swifts.

BIRDTASTICS:
Unusual Behaviour

Great Grey Shrike

Lanius excubitor
LENGTH: 22–26cm WINGSPAN: 30–36cm
FOOD: Birds, small mammals and insects
WHAT IS UNUSUAL? Shrikes impale
large prey on thorny bushes and sharp
branches to make them easier to eat or
to store for later. This behaviour also
helps the male lay claim to its territory
and attract females.

Great Skua

Stercorarius skua
LENGTH: 53–58cm **WINGSPAN:** 125–140cm
FOOD: Fish, birds, small mammals and rodents
FACT: Great Skuas are notorious flying pirates who pester and attack other birds in mid-flight, either as prey or in an effort to make them surrender their own catch.

A GREAT SKUA PURSUES A GANNET.

Treecreeper

Certhia familiaris
LENGTH: 12cm **WINGSPAN:** 18–21cm
FOOD: Insects and spiders
WHAT IS UNUSUAL? As its name suggests, this secretive bird spirals up tree trunks searching for insects living in the bark. They can fly but usually don't go far, typically flying to the base of the next tree to start creeping again.

THERE ARE so many different bird species, it is not surprising to find a wide range of behaviours—some hunt while others eat plants, others migrate while yet more stay in the same place. Within this wide range there are some birds whose behaviour is even more strange or unique than the rest.

FULL TAIL, ROUNDED WHEN IN FLIGHT

SHORT WINGS

CETTI'S WARBLER

Cettia cetti
LENGTH 13.5cm · WINGSPAN 15–19cm · WEIGHT 9–17g
· HABITAT Marshes and wetlands
· FOOD Insects and larvae

THIS ELUSIVE BIRD is one of the UK's most recent colonists, not appearing here until the 1970s. It lacks any showy colours, but has rich dark brown upperparts with a grey-buff chest and pink legs. It is a stocky warbler, usually found around lake edges, marshes and wetlands and is prone to loud bursts of song.

....

LONG-TAILED TIT

Aegithalos caudatus
LENGTH 14cm · WINGSPAN 16–19cm · WEIGHT 7–10g
· HABITAT Farmland, woodland, heathland, parks and gardens · FOOD Insects

WITH ITS PLUMP little body and long tail, this delightful bird is easy to spot in woodland and hedgerows. Look out for its characteristic undulating flight, which means it flies up and down in a wave-like pattern.

TINY BEAK

LONG TAIL

be a BIRD NERD!

Long-tailed Tit nests are vulnerable to predators and often breeding pairs lose their young. When this happens they have been known to help neighbouring breeding pairs raise their chicks instead.

WOOD WARBLER

Phylloscopus sibilatrix
LENGTH 12–13cm · WINGSPAN 19–24cm · WEIGHT 8–12g
· HABITAT Deciduous woodland · FOOD Insects and spiders

THIS WARBLER IS one of the largest in Europe, though still a relatively small bird. It is more brightly coloured than its relatives, and is found in its highest density in the western oak woods of Wales.

BRIGHT YELLOW THROAT

LONG YELLOW STRIPE ABOVE THE EYE

WILLOW WARBLER

Phylloscopus trochilus
LENGTH 10.5–11.5cm · WINGSPAN 16–22cm · WEIGHT 7–12g · HABITAT Grassland, heathland and woodland · FOOD Insects, spiders, fruit and berries

THOUGH VERY SIMILAR to the Chiffchaff, the Willow Warbler has a different melodious song. These are small, delicate birds found across the UK, but especially commonly in Scotland and Ireland.

YELLOW-TINGED CHEST

CHIFFCHAFF

Phylloscopus collybita
LENGTH 10–11cm · WINGSPAN 15–21cm · WEIGHT 6–10g
· HABITAT Lowland parks, gardens and farmland
· FOOD Insects and spiders

THE CHIFFCHAFF IS a summer migrant that looks very like the Willow Warbler except that it has dark-coloured legs. It gets its name from its song—a repetitive *chiff-chaff, chiff-chaff*.

SHORT PALE EYE STRIPE

DARK-COLOURED LEGS

SEDGE WARBLER

Acrocephalus schoenobaenus
LENGTH **13cm** · WINGSPAN **17–21cm**
· WEIGHT **10–13g** · HABITAT **Damp farmland and wetlands** · FOOD **Insects and berries**

THIS WARBLER IS a widely seen summer visitor from Africa. It's not shy or quiet and can often be spotted singing its random song from a bush at the edge of a reedbed. It can be distinguished from other warblers in that it has a slightly bigger body.

POINTY BEAK

CREAM STRIPE ABOVE THE EYE

PLAIN PLUMAGE

REED WARBLER

Acrocephalus scirpaceus
LENGTH **13cm** · WINGSPAN **17–21cm** · WEIGHT **10–15g**
· HABITAT **Reedbeds and wetlands, especially in the south of the UK** · FOOD **Insects and berries**

THIS SUMMER MIGRANT is another plain, relatively small brownish bird with a pale underside. The delicate-looking beak is quite long. They nest only in reed beds—most commonly in East Anglia—and are a major host for the Cuckoo. Listen for the chattering song.

BUFF-COLOURED UNDERSIDE

GRASSHOPPER WARBLER

Locustella naevia
LENGTH 12.5–13.5cm
WINGSPAN 15–19cm   WEIGHT 11–16g
HABITAT Bushy grassland and scrubland,
lightly forested woodland   FOOD Insects

THIS LARGER WARBLER

likely gets its name from its high-pitched, insect-like song, which is usually the first sign of its presence. If seen on the move, this little bird could even be mistaken for a mouse as it scuttles along the ground.

BEAK IS DARK BROWN
ON TOP AND YELLOW-
BROWN ON THE
BOTTOM

be a BIRD NERD!

Even though the Grasshopper Warbler is insectivorous, it doesn't get its name from its food, but instead because its song sounds similar to the noise a grasshopper makes.

10s spotters

PINK LEGS

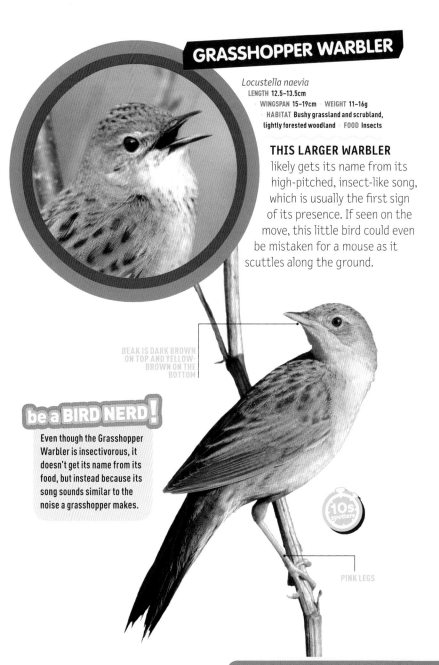

BLACKCAP

Sylvia atricapilla
LENGTH 13cm · **WINGSPAN** 20–23cm · **WEIGHT** 21g
· **HABITAT** Woods, shrubland and wooded
gardens and parks · **FOOD** Insects and berries

THIS HANDSOME WARBLER
has a beautiful song that
lifts the spirits when it
returns to us in spring from
Northern Europe. A few
spend the winter here and
become regular visitors to the
garden and bird table. They
spend a large part of their lives in
thick cover but the singing of the
male gives them away. The female is
similar but with a brown cap.

BLACK CAP
(MALE)

GREY PLUMAGE

GREY/BROWN
PLUMAGE

GARDEN WARBLER

Sylvia borin
LENGTH 14cm · **WINGSPAN** 20–25cm
· **WEIGHT** 16–22g · **HABITAT** Deciduous woodland
· **FOOD** Insects and berries

THIS WARBLER HAS no
distinguishing features—
which could be seen as a
feature in itself. Like the
Blackcap, it has a delightful
song but, unlike its relative—
and rather confusingly given
its name—is not a great
visitor of gardens and bird tables
preferring woodland instead.

PALE BELLY

BLACK
MASK

LESSER WHITETHROAT

Sylvia curruca
LENGTH **13cm** · WINGSPAN **18cm** · WEIGHT **12g**
· HABITAT **Lowland grass and scrubland** · FOOD **Insects and berries**

AS ITS NAME suggests, this is the smaller cousin of the Whitethroat. It rarely flits from cover, but when it does you might catch a glimpse of its white tail feathers. Alternatively, you may hear this bird's harsh *tacking* call.

WHITE OUTER
TAIL FEATHERS

....

WHITETHROAT

Sylvia communis
LENGTH **14cm** · WINGSPAN **18–23cm** · WEIGHT **12–18g**
· HABITAT **Lowland grassland, farmland and wooded areas** · FOOD **Insects and berries**

WITH ITS DISTINCTIVE white throat, this summer migrant is one of the easier warblers to recognise. The male has a grey head while the female's is brown. You might have to venture to the countryside to find it though, as it tends to avoid urban areas.

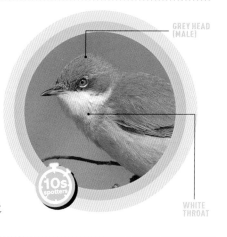

GREY HEAD
(MALE)

WHITE
THROAT

....

PINKISH-RED
BREAST
LONG
TAIL

DARTFORD WARBLER

Sylvia undata
LENGTH **12–13cm** · WINGSPAN **13–18cm** · WEIGHT **9–12g** · HABITAT **Heathland** · FOOD **Insects**

THIS DARK BUT colourful warbler is resident in the UK, although it isn't terribly common. It has increased in number and range since the 1960s, however, when its population had crashed to just a few pairs. Look out for this bird darting between bushes.

ORANGE STRIPE
(MALE)

BRONZE
COLLAR

FIRECREST

Regulus ignicapillus
LENGTH 9cm · **WINGSPAN 13–16cm** · **WEIGHT 5–7g**
**HABITAT Evergreen woodland, hedges
and scrubland, in the south of the country**
FOOD Spiders and small insects

ALONG WITH THE Goldcrest,
this tiny bird is one of the
UK's smallest. It is brighter
and cleaner looking than
its relative, however, with
intricate patterns around
its head and neck. The
Firecrest is a restless species
with lots of energy, and isn't
easily spotted!

THIN, POINTY BEAK

HEAD STRIPE

GOLDCREST

Regulus regulus
LENGTH 9cm · **WINGSPAN 14cm**
WEIGHT 6g · **HABITAT Woodland**
FOOD Small insects, insect eggs and larvae

THIS IS A tiny, greenish-coloured
bird that is usually seen flitting
from branch to branch on
larches and other coniferous
trees. Its thin and pointy beak is
ideal for picking insects from
between pine needles. If you see
one, look for the yellow stripe with
black lines on either side on the
bird's head.

WREN

Troglodytes troglodytes
LENGTH 9–10cm · WINGSPAN 13–17cm
· WEIGHT 7–12g · HABITAT Farmland, heathland
and woods, as well as parks and gardens
· FOOD Insects and spiders

DON'T BE FOOLED by the tiny size of this bird—it is actually one of our loudest! Although you wouldn't miss its call, it can be harder to spot the Wren, as it has a habit of hiding in hedges and holes in banks. This may be the reason behind its Latin name, *Troglodytes*, which means "cavedweller".

SHORT, NARROW TAIL

ROUNDED BODY

be a BIRD NERD!

When it comes to breeding time the male Wren will build the shell of several nests in different locations on his territory. When he attracts a female she then selects the nest that she prefers and completes it by lining the inside. It is not uncommon for the male to then attract further females to some of his other nests!

NUTHATCH

Sitta europaea
LENGTH 14cm · WINGSPAN 22–27cm
· WEIGHT 20–25g · HABITAT Woodland in England and
southern Scotland · FOOD Nuts, seeds and insects

THE NUTHATCH IS distinctive in that it resembles a small woodpecker. In the wild woodland it scrambles around on tree trunks and branches looking for insects. This bird will readily visit garden feeders.

BLUE-GREY
PLUMAGE

LONG,
POINTED
BEAK

STARLING

Sturnus vulgaris

LENGTH 21cm · **WINGSPAN** 37–42cm · **WEIGHT** 75–90g
· **HABITAT** Woodland, parks and gardens
· **FOOD** Insects and fruit

WITH THEIR DISTINCT green and purple plumage Starlings are one of the most recognisable birds you can see. They will nest in any hole they can find, often in hollow trees and they are excellent mimics—imitating phones and alarms are a speciality! While they are still a common sight across the whole country, Starling numbers have dropped quite sharply over the last 50 years. The exact reason for their decline is not known.

POINTED YELLOW BEAK CHANGES TO A DARKER COLOUR IN WINTER

GLOSSY GREEN AND PURPLE FEATHERS

be a BIRD NERD!

In early evening, particularly in autumn, Starlings gather in huge flocks where they fly in fantastic wave formations. These groupings are known as murmurations and can involve many thousands of birds. It is thought that they do this to avoid predators, to keep warm and to exchange information.

DARK PLUMAGE WITH PALER WING PANEL

RING OUZEL

Turdus torquatus
LENGTH 23–24cm · WINGSPAN 38–42cm · WEIGHT 95–130g
· HABITAT **Upland valleys, gullies and rocky crags**
· FOOD **Insects and berries**

SMALLER AND SLIMMER than their Blackbird relatives, Ring Ouzels are upland birds, which means they are usually found on higher ground. They breed in steep-sided valleys, crags and gullies, making mountainous Scotland a perfect home. Here, their nests lie on the ground, often amongst the heather.

WHITE BREAST BAND

YELLOW RING AROUND THE EYE

BLACKBIRD

Turdus merula
LENGTH 24–25cm · WINGSPAN 34–39cm
· WEIGHT 80–100g · HABITAT **Very widespread, found in all habitats and across the country except in the extreme highlands**
· FOOD **Insects, worms and berries**

WITH HIS SHINY black plumage, yellow beak, and yellow ring round his eye, the male Blackbird is a handsome bird. His song is also very musical, and there is even a well-known song named after him! The female is a dark brown colour.

YELLOW BEAK

GREY HEAD

FIELDFARE

Turdus pilaris
LENGTH 25cm · WINGSPAN 39–42cm · WEIGHT 80–130g
HABITAT Grassland and farmland across the country
FOOD Insects, worms and berries

THE FIELDFARE IS a large, colourful thrush. It is a sociable bird, often travelling in large flocks, which sweep the UK countryside in the winter. When not flying with their friends, they may be seen standing very upright, or moving along the ground in hopping movements.

CHESTNUT BACK AND WINGS

CREAM STRIPE ABOVE THE EYE

ORANGE-RED FLANK PATCHES

REDWING

Turdus iliacus
LENGTH 21cm · WINGSPAN 33–35cm
WEIGHT 50–75g · HABITAT Farmland and
hedgerows · FOOD Worms and berries

REDWINGS AREN'T too hard to see as almost 750,000 of them arrive in the UK to overwinter until March. These birds are the smallest members of the thrush family. Large flocks inhabit open fields, eating worms and also berries from the hedgerow.

SONG THRUSH

Turdus philomelos
LENGTH 23cm · WINGSPAN 33–36cm · WEIGHT 65–100g
HABITAT Woods, farmland, parks and gardens
FOOD Invertebrates and fruit

SONG THRUSHES ARE
found in gardens, woods
and hedgerows. The brown
back and speckled breast
make these easy birds
to identify. As the name
suggests, they like to sing,
and sound quite a lot like the
Blackbird, except that they prefer
to repeat song phrases.

SPECKLED
BREAST

PINK LEGS

MISTLE THRUSH

Turdus viscivorus
LENGTH 27cm · WINGSPAN 42–48cm
WEIGHT 100–150g
HABITAT Woodland, parks and gardens
FOOD Invertebrates and fruit

THIS IS OUR largest thrush.
It can be aggressive and
will drive off birds like
Magpies from its territory
if required. It's easy to
spot singing from the top
of a tall tree; its plumage
is slightly greyer than that
of the Song Thrush.

YELLOW-BROWN LEGS

GREYISH/BROWN
PLUMAGE

STRIPED HEAD
PLUMAGE

SPOTTED FLYCATCHER

Muscicapa striata

LENGTH **14cm** · WINGSPAN **23–25cm** · WEIGHT **14–19g** · HABITAT **Farmland, woodland, parks and gardens** · FOOD **Flying insects**

ALTHOUGH SPOTTED

Flycatchers may seem uninteresting at first glance, they are actually captivating little birds. When catching their prey, they can be seen launching themselves from a high perch, grabbing an insect in flight, and then returning to the same spot within seconds. In the UK, these birds nest happily in farmyards, large gardens or open woodland.

PALE CHEST
AND BELLY

ROBIN

BROWN PLUMAGE

Erithacus rubecula

LENGTH **14cm** · WINGSPAN **20–22cm** · WEIGHT **14–21g** · HABITAT **Very widespread in woodland, parks and gardens** · FOOD **Worms, seeds and insects**

PROBABLY THE UK'S most famous and favourite bird, the Robin is best known for its red breast. These birds are very territorial, and although associated with winter, they are year-round residents in the UK.

be a BIRD NERD!

Robins have been found nesting in all kinds of places, but they don't seem to like nest boxes with round entrance holes, so if you want to attract them use open fronted nexting boxes instead.

RED BREAST

NIGHTINGALE

Luscinia megarhynchos
LENGTH 15–17cm · WINGSPAN 23–26cm · WEIGHT 17–24g
· HABITAT Wetlands and grassland with access to water
in southern England · FOOD Insects

NIGHTINGALES LOOK FAIRLY similar to Robins, but are plain brown in colour with a paler breast. They are well known for their complex song, though being secretive, they are hard to spot.

PALE BROWN BREAST

PINK LEGS

SMALL, POINTY BEAK

PIED FLYCATCHER

Ficedula hypoleuca
LENGTH 13cm · WINGSPAN 21–24cm
· WEIGHT 12–15g · HABITAT Woodland
in England and Scotland · FOOD Insects,
caterpillars, seeds and fruit

THE MALE OF the species is black with white markings, while the female is predominantly brown in colour. The Pied Flycatcher does as its name would suggest, and catches flies! It is slightly smaller than the House Sparrow.

WHITE MARKINGS (MALE)

BLACK MASK

ORANGE-RED TAIL

REDSTART

Phoenicurus phoenicurus
LENGTH **14cm** · WINGSPAN **20–24cm** · WEIGHT **11–19g**
HABITAT **Parks, shrubs and coastal woodland**
FOOD **Insects, spiders, worms and berries**

REDSTARTS ARE STRIKING and immediately identifiable, with their bright red chests, black masks and quivering, orange-red tails. These birds move similarly to Robins, with a bobbing motion.

Laugh Out Loud!

Joke: Why did the Redstart fly south for the winter?

Answer: Because it was too far to walk!

. . . .

WHINCHAT

Saxicola rubetra
LENGTH **12.5cm** · WINGSPAN **21–24cm** · WEIGHT **16–24g**
HABITAT **Upland heaths and moorland**
FOOD **Insects and seeds**

THIS SMALL BIRD is a summer visitor to the UK, spending its winters in the warmer surroundings of central and southern Africa. It is often seen perching on the top of low bushes.

WHITE STRIPE ABOVE THE EYE

ORANGE-RED BREAST

STONECHAT

Saxicola rubicola
LENGTH **12.5cm** · WINGSPAN **18–21cm**
· WEIGHT **13–17g** · HABITAT **Heathland,
coniferous woodland and coastal areas**
· FOOD **Invertebrates, seeds and berries**

THIS BIRD GETS its name
from its call, which sounds
like two pebbles being
knocked together. Look
out for its black, white
and orange plumage,
particularly on heaths,
commons and moors.

BLACK HEAD
FEATHERS (MALE)

ORANGE-RED CHEST

GREY BACK

WHEATEAR

Oenanthe oenanthe
LENGTH **14.5–15.5cm** · WINGSPAN **26–32cm** · WEIGHT **17–30g**
· HABITAT **Upland heaths and moorland** · FOOD **Insects**

THESE BIRDS ARE summer
migrants from Africa and
are commonly found on
open moorland. The male
Wheatear has a grey back,
white rump, black face
stripes and orange-pink
chest; the female is paler
and lacks the black cheeks.

be a BIRD NERD!

The name Wheatear does not relate
to the crop or an ear, but comes
instead from an old english slang
term for the bird's white rump!

WHITE RUMP

DIPPER

Cinclus cinclus
LENGTH **18cm** · WINGSPAN **25–30cm**
· WEIGHT **55–75g** HABITAT **Fast-flowing rivers across the country**
· FOOD **Insect larvae and shrimps**

THIS BIRD HAS a low, whirring flight and can often be seen perched, with its short tail cocked in the air. The Dipper is not afraid of water, and in fact will wade into a stream or shallow river in search of food!

BROWN PLUMAGE

WHITE THROAT

SHORT TAIL

BIRDTASTICS: You'll Be Lucky...

Common Rosefinch

Carpodacus erythrinus
LENGTH: 14–15cm
WINGSPAN: 22–26cm
FOOD: Seeds, shoots and invertebrates
BE A BIRD NERD: These pretty little birds are rare visitors to the UK but you might be lucky enough to see one on the south or east coasts in spring or autumn.

MORE THAN 200 different bird species are sighted and recorded across the UK in any single year, but some are much more widely seen than others. While almost everyone can spot a Robin or a Sparrow, you would have to be very lucky indeed to see any of the birds on this page in the wild. Some of them, like the Common (or Scarlet) Rosefinch, pay only fleeting visits as they migrate through the UK, while others, like the Honey Buzzard, have a very small local population.

Honey Buzzard

Pernis apivorus
LENGTH: 52–60cm
WINGSPAN: 135–150cm
FOOD: Larvae of wasps and bees
BE A BIRD NERD: A large bird of prey similar in size to its relative the Buzzard, it's plumage varies according to the bird's age. There are so few nest sites in the UK tha their locations are kept secret.

A SPLENDID HOOPOE PERCHES
ON AN OLD BRANCH BY A LAKE.

Hoopoe

Upupa epops
LENGTH: 25–28cm
WINGSPAN: 42–46cm
FOOD: Insects and spiders
BE A BIRD NERD: These magnificently
decorated birds are such a rare sight
that experts believe they have so far
only come to the UK by mistake!

GREY CAP (MALE)

SHORT, CHUNKY BEAK

HOUSE SPARROW

Passer domesticus
LENGTH 14–15cm · WINGSPAN 21–25.5cm
· WEIGHT 24–38g · HABITAT Woods,
gardens and farmland, across the
country except extreme highlands
· FOOD Seeds and scraps

THIS OFTEN-SEEN and easily recognisable little bird will readily feed on household scraps and seeds from the bird table as well as on insects. Females of the species are dominant, despite being smaller, and can fight over males in breeding season.

....

TREE SPARROW

Passer montanus
LENGTH 14cm · WINGSPAN 20–22cm
· WEIGHT 19–25g · HABITAT Farmland and
woodland · FOOD Seeds and insects

SMALLER THAN the House Sparrow and even more active, the Tree Sparrow is a shy bird that is a lot more difficult to spot in the average garden. You can tell them apart from their bigger relative by their brown caps and the little black spots on their cheeks.

BROWN CAP

BLACK THROAT

POINTY BEAK

GREY ON HEAD AND NECK

10s spotters

DUNNOCK

Prunella modularis
LENGTH 14cm · WINGSPAN 19–21cm · WEIGHT 19–24g
HABITAT Woodland, scrubland and grassland across the country · FOOD Insects, spiders, worms and seeds

OFTEN SEEN AROUND hedges and wrongly called the Hedge Sparrow, the Dunnock is not related to sparrows. These birds are often seen quietly and efficiently picking up scraps under the bird table. Perhaps their only noisy moments occur when two rival males meet and start flicking their wings, calling loudly.

be a BIRD NERD!

Dunnocks are quite unusual amongst birds in that the female often mates with more than one male during the same breeding season. This means that chicks in the same nest can have different fathers.

YELLOW WAGTAIL

Motacilla flava
LENGTH **17cm** · WINGSPAN **23–27cm** · WEIGHT **16–22g** · HABITAT **Lowland grassland, farmland and damp meadows** · FOOD **Insects**

YELLOW WAGTAILS ARE
graceful, slender birds, often found on lowland grassland throughout eastern England, especially where there are cattle grazing. They feed on insects and other small creatures, spending much of their time on the ground.

LONG TAIL

STRIKING YELLOW BREAST

GREY UPPERPARTS

GREY WAGTAIL

Motacilla cinerea
LENGTH **18–19cm** · WINGSPAN **25–27cm** · WEIGHT **14–22g** · HABITAT **Farmland and grassland near streams and rivers** · FOOD **Insects**

GREY WAGTAILS HAVE
conspicuous yellow patches on their breasts and rumps. They can be found right across the country, but prefer being close to water and are often found nesting by fast-flowing streams or under bridges.

YELLOW RUMP

PIED WAGTAIL

Motacilla alba

LENGTH 18cm · WINGSPAN 25–30cm · WEIGHT 17–25g
HABITAT Most areas, especially near water
FOOD Insects

THE PIED WAGTAIL is not just a countryside bird, and it often roosts in large numbers in cities. Its black and white plumage makes this bird hard to miss. It's always rushing about flicking its tail while searching for insects.

WHITE MASK

SMALL, POINTY BEAK

MEADOW PIPIT

Anthus pratensis

LENGTH 14.5cm · WINGSPAN 22–25cm
WEIGHT 15–22g · HABITAT Meadows, moorland,
farmland and coastal wetlands and marshes
FOOD Insects and spiders

YOU CAN PROBABLY tell from the name that this bird is usually found in open grassland or moorland. It is a small brown bird with a fairly long tail, which it flicks as it runs along the ground.

PINK LEGS

PALE SUPERCILIUM
(STRIPE ABOVE THE EYE)

TREE PIPIT

Anthus trivialis
LENGTH 15cm · WINGSPAN 25–27cm · WEIGHT 20–25g
HABITAT Grassland, heathland and light woodland
FOOD Small invertebrates and berries

OFTEN MISTAKEN FOR a Thrush, the Tree Pipit sings as it flies from perch to perch. It's a common summer visitor and populates our heath, moorland and young tree plantations, eating small insects and berries.

PALE PINK LEGS

OLIVE-BROWN PLUMAGE

ROCK PIPIT

Anthus petrosus
LENGTH 16.5cm · WINGSPAN 23–28cm
WEIGHT 20–30g · HABITAT Rocky
shorelines · FOOD Insects, small fish

ALTHOUGH SIMILAR IN colouring, this pipit is larger and stockier than its Meadow relative. They are most likely to be seen at the coast, particularly on rocky beaches, where they breed and reside, or visit from Norway for the winter.

BROWN LEGS

RED MASK AND
CHEST (MALE)

FORKED TAIL

CHAFFINCH

Fringilla coelebs
LENGTH 14.5cm · WINGSPAN 24–28.5cm · WEIGHT 18–29g
· HABITAT Woodland, heathland, hedges, gardens
and parks · FOOD Insects and seeds

THE FIRST SIGN of a
Chaffinch is usually its loud
song and varied calls. It is a
common bird in the UK, and
can be seen in gardens,
though it prefers not to feed
openly but to hop around
under tables or hedges
instead. Its patterned plumage
is attractive and distinctive.

ORANGE
BREAST

WHITE RUMP

BRAMBLING

Fringilla montifringilla
LENGTH 14cm · WINGSPAN 25–26cm · WEIGHT 24g
· HABITAT Woodland, farmland and wooded gardens
· FOOD Seeds and insects

THE BRAMBLING IS a
friend of the Chaffinch, with
whom it is often seen in
large mixed flocks. This bird
is a colourful finch, and more
than a million of them arrive in
the UK in late September every
year.

ORANGE HEAD

HAWFINCH

Coccothraustes coccothraustes
LENGTH 18cm · WINGSPAN 29–33cm
· WEIGHT 48–62g · HABITAT Woodland and
parks · FOOD Seeds, buds and shoots

THIS BIRD IS the largest finch found in the UK, though it is a shy species and therefore difficult to spot. Its most recognisable feature has to be its beak, which is massive compared to its body and can exert impressive force.

LARGE, CHUNKY BEAK

....

BULLFINCH

Pyrrhula pyrrhula
LENGTH 14.5–16.5cm · WINGSPAN 22–26cm · WEIGHT 21–27g
· HABITAT Woodland, fruit orchards and hedges
· FOOD Seeds, buds and insects

THIS GLORIOUSLY pink-red male and the creamy-yellow breasted female were once common and well known pests in fruit orchards, feeding on buds, seeds and insects. The Bullfinch is now, however, on the RSPB Red List due to habitat decline and modern pesticides used by farmers. Resident Bullfinches usually stay close to home, rarely travelling more than a few kilometres from where they hatch.

BLACK CAP AND MASK

PINKISH-RED BREAST AND THROAT (MALE)

YELLOWISH-GREEN PLUMAGE

GREENFINCH

Carduelis chloris
LENGTH 15cm   WINGSPAN 26cm   WEIGHT 28g   HABITAT Woodland, hedges and gardens   FOOD Seeds and insects

ALTHOUGH NOT quite as numerous as the Chaffinch, you can find Greenfinches across the whole country. Look for them in woods, along hedgerows, in parks, but also in your garden. The male bird is a bright yellowish green while the female is rather duller.

YELLOW WING EDGE

TWITE

Carduelis flavirostris
LENGTH 14cm   WINGSPAN 22–24cm   WEIGHT 13–18g   HABITAT Moorland, wetlands and coastal grassland   FOOD Seeds

TWITES ARE SMALL finches, fairly similar to their Linnet cousins, though rarer. They breed on the fringes of moorlands in northern England and Scotland.

LONG TAIL

STUBBY BEAK

be a BIRD NERD!

The Twite gets its name from its distinctinve call which is made up of lots of fast *twit* sounds.

PINKISH-RED BREAST (MALE: SUMMER)

GREY HEAD

LINNET

Carduelis cannabina

LENGTH **13.5cm** · WINGSPAN **21–26cm** · WEIGHT **15–22g** · HABITAT **Heathland, commons, wetlands, parks and gardens** · FOOD **Seeds and insects**

THESE BIRDS ARE found in open country where there are trees and bushes. Linnets are greyish brown above and paler on the underside but, in spring and summer, the chest of the male bird is flushed with pink. Numbers have declined over the last few decades so that it is now on the Red List.

RED HEAD PATCH

LESSER REDPOLL

Carduelis cabaret

LENGTH **11.5cm** · WINGSPAN **20–22.5cm** · WEIGHT **9–12g** · HABITAT **Woods and gardens** · FOOD **Seeds and plants**

THE LESSER REDPOLL is less well known than the bigger finches but can often be seen in gardens hanging upside down to feed. Look out for the red strip on the front of this little finch's head and its black chin. In the breeding season the male's breast gets a pink tinge to it. You can find Lesser Redpolls across the country but they are more common in the north.

STREAKY PLUMAGE

SCOTTISH CROSSBILL

Loxia scotica
LENGTH **16–17cm** · WINGSPAN **27–37cm**
· WEIGHT **44g** · HABITAT **Pine forests
in Scotland** · FOOD **Pine seeds**

BOTH SEXES OF this finch
have the characteristic
crossbill, but the male has a
vivid red, patterned plumage
while the female is yellow-
green. There are less than
10,000 breeding pairs, all
located in the north of
Scotland.

LARGE HEAD

RED-ORANGE
PLUMAGE (MALE)

CROSSBILL

10s
spotters

be a BIRD NERD!
The outstanding fact about this finch is that it is the UK's only endemic
bird species, which means it is found nowhere else in the world!

CROSSBILL

Loxia curvirostra
LENGTH 16.5cm · WINGSPAN 27–30cm
WEIGHT 35–50g · HABITAT Conifer forests
FOOD Conifer seeds

THIS BIRD IS hard to tell apart from its cousins, the Scottish Crossbill and Parrot Crossbill. They all have the distinct crossed over beak which helps them extract seeds from conifer cones, but the Crossbill beak is slightly smaller than that of the Scottish or Parrot varieties. They also have slightly different calls. The female has green-brown plumage, while the male is red.

BRIGHT RED FACE

GOLDFINCH

Carduelis carduelis
LENGTH 12cm · WINGSPAN 21–25cm · WEIGHT 14–19g
HABITAT Light woodland, heathland, parks and gardens
FOOD Seeds and insects

THIS DELIGHTFUL LITTLE finch is often seen feeding on the seeds of thistle heads in autumn although it will happily visit a garden feeder too. Its bright red, white, black, and yellow colours make it easy to recognise. Goldfinch numbers in the UK can reach over 1 million pairs in the summer, but while some stay, many migrate to continental Europe for the winter.

YELLOW WING PATCH

SISKIN

Carduelis spinus
LENGTH 12cm · WINGSPAN 20–23cm · WEIGHT 12–18g
HABITAT Forests, wooded gardens and parks
FOOD Seeds and insects

THE SISKIN LOOKS rather like a Greenfinch, except that the male Siskin has a black crown and chin and rather more yellow colours on the underside. These birds eat the seeds of cones.

Laugh Out Loud!

Joke: What do you give a sick bird?

Answer: Tweetment!

YELLOW TAIL PATCHES

BLACK CROWN (MALE)

STREAKY BODY

10s spotters

MOTTLED PLUMAGE (WINTER)

SNOW BUNTING

Plectrophenax nivalis
LENGTH 16–17cm · WINGSPAN 32–38cm
· WEIGHT 28–50g · HABITAT Coastal regions,
particularly in Scotland and eastern England
· FOOD Seeds and insects

THESE ARE LARGE buntings, with striking "snowy" plumages. Aptly, they breed around the arctic from Scandinavia to Alaska, Canada and Greenland, with just a few pairs breeding in the UK. They are more widespread in winter.

BROWN COLLAR

CORN BUNTING

SHORT BEAK

Emberiza calandra
LENGTH 18cm · WINGSPAN 26–32cm · WEIGHT 35–56g
· HABITAT Grassland, farmland and hedges
· FOOD Seeds and insects

THE CORN BUNTING has an interesting song, which sounds like the rattling of a bunch of keys after a *chinkchink* start. In terms of appearance, it is rather similar to the Yellowhammer but without the bright yellow colours.

BROWN STREAKS

YELLOW HEAD
(MALE)

YELLOWHAMMER

Emberiza citrinella
LENGTH 16–16.5cm · WINGSPAN 23–29.5cm
· WEIGHT 25–36g · HABITAT Open countryside,
bushes and hedges · FOOD Seeds and insects

IT IS THE bright yellow head of the male bird which is easy to spot. Listen to his song in spring and summer, as he sits atop a hedge or gate post.

PINKISH-
BROWN
LEGS

REED BUNTING

Emberiza schoeniclus
LENGTH 15–16.5cm · WINGSPAN 21–28cm
· WEIGHT 16–25g · HABITAT Wetlands,
reedbeds and farmland
· FOOD Seeds and insects

THIS BIRD LIVES in wetlands and nests in plants along the water's edge. In the breeding season, it is often to be seen at the top of a reed or bulrush stem, singing loudly. It feeds on both seeds and insects.

BLACK HEAD
(MALE)

WHITE BREAST

Glossary

BAR: A striped pattern, usually made by wing feathers.

BARRED: A heavily striped pattern.

BEAK: Also known as bill; the outside covering of a bird's jaw.

BILL: Also known as beak; the outside covering of a bird's jaw.

BOREAL FOREST: An ecological area characterized by coniferous forests.

BROOD: A new family of baby birds.

BUFF: Tan- or beige-coloured.

CALL: Bird sounds that are shorter than a song and seem to convey a specific message, like an alarm. Listen for *chip* or *kerr*.

CARRION: Dead animals.

CLUTCH: The group of eggs laid in a nest at one time.

COLONY: A large group of birds that nests close together.

CONIFEROUS: Trees that produce cones and have green leaves all year round.

DECIDUOUS: Trees that have leaves that fall off every year.

ESTUARY: A river mouth with mudflats that provide a rich feeding ground for birds.

EXTINCT: No longer existing.

FLOCK: A group of birds, sometimes of the same species, assembled together.

FLUSH: To surprise a group of birds, usually out of bushes, into noisy flight.

INVERTEBRATE: An animal that lacks a spinal column.

IRIDESCENT: Shining with different colours— sometimes producing a rainbow effect when seen from different angles.

JUVENILE: A young bird wearing its first coat of feathers that isn't down.

LEAF LITTER: Pieces of dead plant that cover the ground and are used for making nests.

MIGRATION: Regular movement of birds from one area to another.

MOLTING: The replacement of old feathers with new feathers.

MOTTLED: Speckled plumage.

NESTLINGS: Babies that have not yet left the nest.

OFFSPRING: The young of a bird.

PLUMAGE: All the feathers that cover a bird's body.

PREDATOR: An animal that preys on another animal.

PREENING: The process a bird uses to clean, arrange, and care for its feathers, usually using its beak.

PREY: An animal that is hunted or killed by another animal for food.

REGURGITATE: To bring up food that was swallowed back into the mouth.

ROOST: To sleep, or the place where a bird sleeps.

RUDDER: The flat piece of wood at the rear of a boat that helps steer it. Birds use their tails and wings as rudders.

SCIENTIFIC NAME: A two-word designation for an animal or plant indicating genus and species.

SONG: A pattern of notes, usually produced by males to attract mates or defend a territory.

SONGBIRD: A bird with a complex voice box that can sing more complicated songs than other bird species.

SUET: Beef fat that is easily digested by birds and is high-energy food.

TAIL FEATHERS: Feathers that assist with flight and help a bird make quick turns.

TALONS: Sharp claws for grasping prey.

TUNDRA: Vast, treeless plains in the Arctic region.

UNDERPARTS: The underside of the bird, from its neck and chest to its legs.

UNPPERPARTS: The back of the bird, from head to tail.

VOICE: All the sounds a bird makes. Its voice includes its songs and calls.

WETLANDS: Swamps or marshes.

WING BARS: One or two coloured bars that run across a bird's wing.

Index

PUFFIN p. 63

ROBIN p. 103

Staff for This Book
Amy Briggs, Priyanka Sherman, *Senior Editors*
Jim Hiscott, *Art Director*
Lori Epstein, *Senior Photo Editor*
Angela Modany, *Assistant Editor*
Paige Towler, *Editorial Assistant*
Sanjida Rashid and Rachel Kenny, *Design
   Production Assistants*
Tammi Colleary-Loach, *Rights Clearance Manager*
Michael Cassady and Mari Robinson, *Rights
   Clearance Specialists*
Grace Hill, *Managing Editor*
Alix Inchausti, *Production Editor*
Joan Gossett, *Senior Production Editor*
Lewis R. Bassford, *Production Manager*
Jennifer Hoff, *Manager, Production Services*
Susan Borke, *Legal and Business Affairs*

Produced by Potomac Global Media, LLC
Kevin Mulroy, *Publisher*
Barbara Brownell Grogan, *Editorial Director*
Julie Beer, *Author*
Jonathan Alderfer, *Editorial Consultant*
Bea Jackson, *Art Director*
Project Design Company, *Contributing Designer*
David Hicks, *Picture Editor*
Catherine Howell, Jahanna Beecham, Jane Sunderland,
   Consulting Editors
Tim Griffin, *Indexer*

Published by the National Geographic Society
Gary E. Knell, *President and CEO*
John M. Fahey, *Chairman of the Board*
Melina Gerosa Bellows, *Chief Education Officer*
Declan Moore, *Chief Media Officer*
Hector Sierra, *Senior Vice President and General
   Manager, Book Division*

Senior Management Team, Kids Publishing and Media
Nancy Laties Feresten, *Senior Vice President*
Erica Green, *Vice President, Editorial Director,
   Kids Books*
Amanda Larsen, *Design Director, Kids Books*
Julie Vosburgh Agnone, *Vice President, Operations*
Jennifer Emmett, *Vice President, Content*
Michelle Sullivan, *Vice President, Video and Digital
   Initiatives*
Eva Absher-Schantz, *Vice President, Visual Identity*
Rachel Buchholz, *Editor and Vice President,
   NG Kids magazine*
Jay Sumner, *Photo Director*
Hannah August, *Marketing Director*
R. Gary Colbert, *Production Director*

British English edition
Laura Waddell, *Publishing Manager*
Keith Moore, *Editorial Lead*
Mark Steward, *Design and layout*
Hannah MacAskill, Karen Midgley, Alison James,
   Lauren Murray, Julianna Dunn, *Editors*

Published by Collins
An imprint of HarperCollins Publishers
Westerhill Road
Bishopbriggs
Glasgow G64 2QT
www.harpercollins.co.uk

In association with National Geographic Partners, LLC

Second edition 2019
First published 2016

ISBN 978-0-00-832115-4

10 9 8 7 6 5 4 3 2 1

If you would like to comment on any aspect of this book,
please contact us at the above address or online.
natgeokidsbooks.co.uk
collins.reference@harpercollins.co.uk

Since 1888, the National Geographic Society has funded
more than 12,000 research, exploration, and preservation
projects around the world. The Society receives funds from
National Geographic Partners, LLC, funded in part by your
purchase. A portion of the proceeds from this book supports
this vital work. To learn more, visit natgeo.com/info.